GRAND PRIX
CHAMPIONS

GRAND PRIX CHAMPIONS

FROM JACKIE STEWART TO MICHAEL SCHUMACHER

ALAN HENRY

WEIDENFELD & NICOLSON
LONDON

CONTENTS

INTRODUCTION

Man's intriguing love affair with the internal combustion engine has become one of the most fascinating, some would say inexplicable, aspects of the 20th century. Yet from the moment the first horseless carriages flickered into life, it was perhaps only inevitable that they would spark a competitive spirit and there would soon be plans to race these new-fangled machines.

Scarcely one hundred years have passed since Count de Dion, driving a car which bore his own name, won a reliability run between Paris and Rouen in what has come to be generally regarded as the first proper motorized competition. The sport's first 'Grand Prize' did not take place until 1906 and much competition occurred amidst clouds of dust on unpaved roads until well into the third decade of the century.

Yet, up to the edge of the 1970s, Grand Prix motor racing remained a largely specialized sport. It was funded from within, by motor industry sources - the tyre, fuel and associated component manufacturers. It could be rough, ready, unyielding and downright dangerous.

Then Jackie Stewart came along to change all that. Motor racing, he reasoned, was a job in which the participants were paid to demonstrate their skills - not face an overwhelming, and unreasonably balanced, chance of death or injury. His crusades for improved motor racing safety can be seen as only one element of his legacy to the sport in which his talent shone so brightly.

More than any other single individual, Stewart triggered the cult of the millionaire World Champion, relentlessly promoting commercial business opportunities on the back of his achievements out on the circuit. The death of his compatriot Jim Clark in 1968 is now seen as the end of what might best be called Grand Prix racing's sporting era; thereafter the business became more ruthless and commercially dependent - but also more dazzlingly colourful and competitive than ever before.

This book is about a small group of elite sportsmen who not only conquered their chosen profession, but became world-renowned stars and millionaire businessmen as a direct result. The names of Stewart, Lauda, Prost, Senna, Mansell and Schumacher are associated not only with their Grand Prix champion stature, but with international fame on a wider scale acknowledged in the same breath as Becker, Norman, Graf or Platini.

Today, World Championship Grand Prix motor racing is one of the most slickly presented, avidly followed and well-funded of all the internationally televised sports. And the men you will meet in the pages of this book have become the undisputed Stars of the Show.

ALAN HENRY

PAST, PRESENT AND FUTURE
CHAMPIONS? ALAIN PROST (LEFT)
IN THE COMPANY OF MICHAEL
SCHUMACHER (CENTRE) AND
DAMON HILL (RIGHT) DURING THE
1983 MONACO GRAND PRIX
WEEKEND. WILL HILL JOIN THE
EXCLUSIVE TITLE-HOLDER ELITE IN
1995?

RIGHT: STEWART'S FAMILIAR TARTAN HELMET REMAINS HIS DISTINCTIVE TRADEMARK TO THIS DAY.

JACKIE STEWART, 1994. THREE WORLD CHAMPIONSHIPS, 29 YEARS AND 25 GRAND PRIX WINS LATER, HE IS A MILLIONAIRE BUSINESSMAN WITH A WIDE VARIETY OF INTERESTS ACROSS THE GLOBE.

Jackie Stewart was, in so many ways, the Man Who Made The Difference. His professional motor racing career began in 1962, a time when the effects of the devil-may-care post-war era were still in full flight. The members of that particular motor racing generation, who had survived the 1939–45 conflict, willingly entered a sport which was still potentially just as hazardous as flying a Spitfire at the height of the Battle of Britain. Truth be told, some went motor racing simply because they hankered for a similar cocktail of fear, danger and exhilaration. But John Young Stewart changed all that.

This jaunty, energetic son of a Scottish garage owner from Dumbuck, one of Glasgow's western suburbs, was not simply one of the greatest drivers of his era. Winning three World Championships during a nine-year Formula 1 career was only part of his achievement – Jackie was responsible for de-bunking the image of racing drivers as reckless extroverts.

Almost singlehandedly, he was responsible for initiating far-reaching improvements in circuit safety, and the benefits of his action endure to this day. And, he astutely concluded that Grand Prix stardom could be extended after racing as a platform-for-life. As a businessman, consultant and media personality, more than 20 years after he retired from the cockpit, Jackie is a multi-millionaire with homes in Switzerland and North America. He is one of the most influential and well-connected personalities both in the sport and the international motor industry. In short, he is a household name.

Stewart has certainly trodden a long and varied road since his birth in Dumbarton on the eve of the Second World War, on 11 June, 1939. Academically he was written off at an early age and it was many years before he was identified as suffering from dyslexia.

He is currently a Patron of the Dyslexia Foundation, President of the Scottish Dyslexia Trust and a Trustee of the Dyslexia Institute Scottish Bursary Fund.

Even so, Jackie managed to shrug aside the problems stemming from this disability and became a gifted sportsman at a young age. Between 1959 and 1962 he won the British, Scottish, Irish, Welsh and English trap shooting championship - narrowly failing to be selected for the British Olympic team in 1960.

"I think the difficulties at school gave me a determination to succeed because, amongst

STEWART AND **BRM**, 1965. THE OUTWARD TRACE OF ANY COMMERCIAL SPONSORSHIP IS THE **D**UNLOP LETTERING ON HIS BLUE RACING OVERALLS.

my peers, I'd been shown up to be stupid, dumb and thick at a time when schooling was such a very central, essential part of your life", he reflects with characteristic self-analysis.

"I left school at the age of 15 and served petrol in the family garage for a year. I earned more in the way of tips than I did from my main wages, but I ran the best forecourt in the county. Then I went into the lubrication bay, and made sure you could eat your breakfast off the floor! That was good experience, because for the first time people praised me."

In addition to self-confidence, Stewart acquired the vital skill of discipline. "When I started shooting at the age of 14, I was suddenly provided with something at which I could excel. Those years were enormously

important for the formation of my thinking processes in dealing with competition, with success and with failure."

By this stage, motor racing was already a key factor within the Stewart family. Jackie's elder brother Jimmy had established himself as an accomplished semi-professional driver in the mid-1950s. He was eventually good enough to drive for Ecurie Ecosse, the famous Edinburgh-based team, and the factory Aston Martin and Jaguar squads. After a serious accident in the mid-1950s he retired only for Jackie, who'd had his first taste of opposite-lock motoring in his early teens when he took an elderly Auston 16 for a tentative outing on

BY THIS STAGE, MOTOR RACING WAS ALREADY A KEY FACTOR WITHIN THE STEWART FAMILY

the snow-covered lanes near the family's Dumbuck garage.

The fuse was lit. Jackie had his first motor race at Charterhall, the Scottish airfield circuit, in 1962 at the age of 23. The following year he too drove for Ecurie Ecosse in a Cooper-Monaco sports car and his talent was recognized by the very shrewd Ken Tyrrell. He was invited to drive Tyrrell's Cooper-BMCs in the British Formula 3 championship in 1964 and immediately established a solid reputation as a potential Grand Prix driver.

After dominating this key junior league single-seater category, Jackie found himself on the horns of a dilemma. The legendary Lotus team boss, Colin Chapman, then at the absolute zenith of his achievement, offered him a place in his Grand Prix line-up for 1965 alongside fellow Scot Jim Clark. Jackie declined. It was a shrewd decision.

Stewart could see only too well that

JACKIE STEWART IN THE COCKPIT OF THE BHM H-16 JUST PRIOR TO THE START OF THE 1967 INTERNATIONAL TROPHY MEETING AT SILVERSTONE. IT WAS AN AGE BEFORE THE GREAT COMMERCIAL EXPLOSION WHICH ROCKETED FORMULA 1 RACING TO A POSITION OF INTERNATIONAL TELEVISED PROMINENCE.

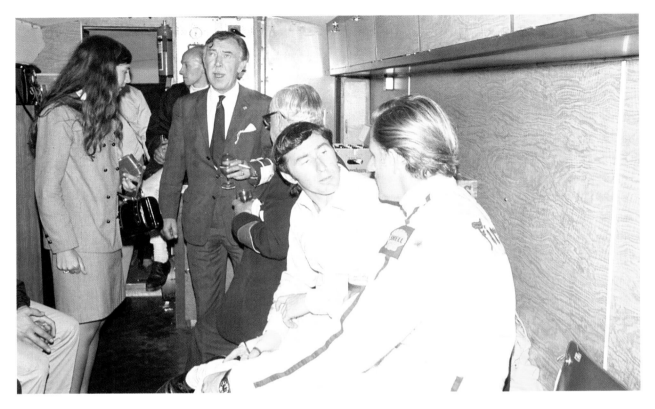

SILVERSTONE IN 1968. STEWART (SECOND FROM RIGHT) CHATS WITH GRAHAM HILL, WHO IS FATHER OF TODAY'S F1 STAR DAMON. HILL SENIOR IS SLAKING HIS THIRST WITH A PINT; A GENERATION LATER, HIS SON WOULD PREFER CAMOMILE TEA OR MINERAL WATER AS HIS RACE-DAY TIPPLE!

Clark's role as unchallenged number one driver at Lotus would leave him with a disadvantage. At that time, the role of Lotus number two drivers had not been a happy one. Jackie had no intention of being eclipsed in such a fashion and, instead, signed to drive for the BRM team alongside Graham Hill. It was a perspicacious move which helped him to quickly establish himself as the most promising newcomer in the Formula 1 game.

Even so, he had his first F1 outing guest-driving for Team Lotus in the non-championship Rand Grand Prix held at Johannesburg's Kyalami circuit in December 1964, emphasizing his potential by starting from pole position. Little more than a month later, he was back in South Africa to score a Championship point for sixth place on his maiden outing with the BRM team at East London.

Back to Europe and he qualified the BRM on pole position for the non-title race at Goodwood and then won the Silverstone International Trophy race, beating Ferrari's John Surtees – then the reigning World Champion – into second place. Later that very same season his status as a rising star was cemented when he won the 1965 Italian Grand Prix at Monza, out-fumbling his team-mate Graham Hill in a last-lap sprint to the chequered flag.

The following year, Jackie started out on a high note by winning the Monaco Grand Prix in a 2-litre BRM, but the onset of the 3-litre F1 regulations left the British team grappling with seemingly insolvable technical problems. But 1966 was also responsible for shaping Jackie's trenchant views on the subject of motor racing safety after he crashed in heavy rain during the Belgian Grand Prix on the daunting Spa-Francorchamps road circuit.

...HIS STATUS AS A RISING STAR WAS CEMENTED WHEN HE WON THE **1965** ITALIAN GRAND PRIX AT MONZA...

IT IS ALL A FAR CRY FROM THE 1969 SOUTH AFRICAN GRAND PRIX WHICH HE WON IN THIS TYRELL TEAM MATRA-FORD, THE START OF A SUCCESSFUL SEASON'S CAMPAIGN TO WIN THE FIRST OF HIS THREE WORLD CHAMPIONSHIPS.

For those more accustomed to the neatly manicured track edges and generous gravel run-off areas which are the hallmark of modern-day Grand Prix circuits, Jackie's description of the accident seems incredibly brutal, something out of the Stone Age.

"I must have been doing around 165 mph when the car began aquaplaning and I lost control", he winces. "First I hit a telegraph pole, then a woodcutter's cottage and finished up in the outside basement of a farm building. The car ended up shaped like a banana and I was still trapped inside it. The fuel tank had ruptured inwardly and the chassis was literally filling up with fuel. It was sloshing around inside the cockpit. The instrument panel was smashed, ripped off and found 200 metres away. But the electric fuel pump was still working away, the steering wheel wouldn't come off and I couldn't get out."

A spark would almost certainly have caused a fatal fire. Under the circumstances,

JACKIE STEWART'S TYRELL-FORD LEADS CLAY REGAZZONI'S BRM AND THE LOTUS 72 OF EMERSON FITTIPALDI IN THE 1973 ARGENTINE GRAND PRIX AT BUENOS AIRES. IT WOULD BE THE SCOT'S FINAL SEASON BEFORE RETIREMENT AT THE AGE OF 34.

BELOW: TWO CHAMPIONS TOGETHER. JACKIE IN THE COMPANY OF MARIO ANDRETTI, TITLE WINNER IN 1978 AND JUST AS SHREWD A BUSINESSMAN IN EVERY WAY.

it could be seen as amazing that Stewart survived at all; in those days, no F1 driver wore seat belts. But he survived with several broken ribs, shoulder and pelvic injuries and was back racing again within a few weeks. Jackie's commitment to motor racing safety moved into pin-sharp focus, and it has remained so to this day.

Even at this relatively early stage in his career, Jackie and his wife Helen moved into tax exile in Switzerland. During that maiden 1965 season with BRM he had been paid a fee of £10,000. Small beer by today's standards, perhaps, but serious money 30 years ago, at a time when a successful solicitor might take home around £4,000 and live in conditions of extreme comfort. Jackie cites the Labour

JACKIE AND HIS WIFE HELEN IN 1993.

government's punitive rates of marginal taxation as the main reason for his move. Yet it is hard to imagine Stewart still living in Scotland today. Even by the late 1960s it was clear that the garage owner's son was set on becoming a Citizen of the World.

After the Spa accident, Jackie never raced a car without seat belts. In addition, he would equip himself with the best helmets, and always the state-of-the art flameproof overalls. The die-hard traditionalists attacked his circuit safety crusade as namby-pamby stuff. But he was ahead of his time – and the most convincing justification for his standpoint was the fact that he developed into a consistent race winner.

By the end of 1967 he decided to turn his back on the fast-fading BRM team. Jackie accepted an invitation to drive for Ken Tyrrell's new F1 squad, using superbly crafted chassis built by the French Matra aerospace company powered by Ford Cosworth V8 engines. He just missed out on the 1968 World Championship to Graham Hill, but stormed to the 1969 title in brilliant style.

Those who thought Stewart a bit soft would do well to recall the 1968 Belgian Grand Prix. Only two years after that terrible accident on the same track, Jackie and the Tyrrell Matra were the class of the field – despite the fact that he was driving with a broken bone in one wrist which was strapped up in a plastic cast! He was deprived of victory only when the Matra ran short of fuel

JACKIE'S SON PAUL RACED PROFESSIONALLY FROM THE LATE 1980S THROUGH TO HIS RETIREMENT AT THE END OF 1993. HERE HE RECEIVES A FEW TIPS FROM HIS FATHER.

in the closing stages of the race.

By now Stewart had shed his close-cropped, conservative Scottish image. His hair now flowed over his collar in suitable sixties style to cause further offence to the stuffed-shirt brigade. But he was winning, winning, winning. In 1970, Tyrrell switched briefly to the uncompetitive March chassis, then built his own Ford-engined car. Jackie won the championship again in 1971 and 1973. Then he decided it was time to hang up his helmet at the young age of 34.

BY THE TIME HE STOPPED RACING, JACKIE HAD WON NO FEWER THAN 27 GRANDS PRIX...

He was already a millionaire, socially well connected and with a portfolio of business clients to underpin his commercial life long after the roar of the final exhaust had faded. Princess Anne attended his retirement party and Helen Stewart was later asked to be godmother to her daughter Zara.

By the time he stopped racing, Jackie had won no fewer than 27 Grands Prix, an all-time record which would endure for another 14 years before being beaten by Frenchman Alain Prost.

A shrewd awareness that high quality companies would only do business with like-minded individuals proved the key factor which enabled Jackie Stewart to expand his original sporting career to a much wider commercial arena. The uncompromising attention to detail and absolute commitment he brought to bear on his career as a professional racing driver was now applied to his position as an international businessman. By the time his racing career finished, his overall income was running in the order of $1 million a year and, even by the mid-1980s, there were only a handful of active top Grand Prix drivers who earned more than the long-retired Scot.

Whether lecturing young businessmen on the merits of promptly answering telephone calls, developing his shooting school at Scotland's prestigious Gleneagles Hotel or commuting across the Atlantic on Concorde in the way mere mortals would use a number seven bus, Jackie Stewart remains at the forefront of the international social and business scene. His motor racing links also remain as firmly established as ever through his son Paul's highly professional British-based team, which competes in both the Formula 3 and 3000 international single-seater categories.

He also retains two matchless gifts – a sense of humour and the ability to laugh at himself. Small wonder that Jackie Stewart's standing within the Grand Prix community remains so high, more than two decades after hanging up that distinctive white helmet with the tartan band for the last time.

SHARING THE CHAMPAGNE WITH TOP TEAM BOSS FRANK WILLIAMS AT JACKIE'S SHOOTING SCHOOL AT SCOTLAND'S PRESTIGIOUS GLENEAGLES HOTEL – JUST ONE OF THE HIGH-QUALITY BUSINESS PROJECTS WITH WHICH HE HAS BECOME ASSOCIATED IN HIS POST-RACING LIFE.

Emerson Fittipaldi established a Brazilian beachhead in front-line European motor racing at the start of the 1970s, and since that time many of his compatriots have poured into the sport. Yet when this son of a São Paulo motor racing journalist and commentator made his F1 debut at Brands Hatch in the 1970 British Grand Prix, he could hardly have imagined that his racing career would still be running at full blast a quarter of a century later.

Emerson may have turned his back on F1 in 1980 when his family team closed its doors, but in the years that followed he dramatically rejuvenated himself with a switch to the US domestic Indycar series. Not only has he won the F1 World Championship twice, but he followed that up with matching wins in the Indianapolis 500 classic in 1989 and 1993. Not even the legendary Jim Clark, who won both Indy and the F1 title back in 1965, managed to take two wins in both of these glitteringly prestigious contests.

Fittipaldi also became the youngest F1 World Champion ever with his 1972 win at the age of 25. With little more than a dozen Grands Prix under his belt, Emerson had only won a single race prior to his title season. Two years earlier he had made his tentative F1 debut as a junior member of Colin Chapman's famous Lotus squad, but within weeks its team leader Jochen Rindt, the mercurial Austrian star, was killed during practice for the Italian Grand Prix at Monza. This left Emerson suddenly propelled into *de facto* team leadership and, aided by a

timely slice of good fortune, he emerged triumphant from the 1970 United States Grand Prix – only his fourth Formula 1 race. It was a quite remarkably cool performance from the young Brazilian, the disadvantage was that it raised unrealistically optimistic hopes for the Lotus level of achievement the following year.

Truth be told, Emerson was still learning his craft. His progress through the junior single-seater formulae had been meteoric; his rare blend of speed and precision proved ideal for extracting the best out of the modestly-powered Formula Ford and F3 machinery on which he cut his teeth. His talent was obvious and enduring, but Grand Prix success would have to wait while he expanded on his personal reserves of race strategy, experience and judgement.

As a result, 1971 proved something of a transitional year. The Lotus 72, a pace setter the previous season, lagged slightly in terms of technical development. Fittipaldi's season was also punctuated by a road accident in which he sustained several broken ribs. Yet it was a measure of his steely determination that Emerson drove to a strong third place in the French Grand Prix and finished the season a slightly disappointed sixth overall in the Drivers' World Championship.

Everything gelled perfectly, however, in 1972. The Lotus 72 was tuned to a fresh pitch of technical excellence. Emerson had the experience to get the job done and Chapman clearly had the confidence in his ability. He surged to five commanding victories, which saw him clinch the Championship at Monza, only two years after the Lotus team was left in the depths of despair by Rindt's death.

Emerson Fittipaldi's fame in his native land was such that Brazil hosted its first contemporary Formula 1 race at the start of 1972, albeit a non-championship affair, at São Paulo's Interlagos circuit. Lotus sent a

FITTIPALDI WON THE FIRST OF HIS TWO WORLD CHAMPIONSHIPS IN THIS BLACK AND GOLD, JPS-LIVERIED LOTUS 72.

EMERSON FITTIPALDI WAS STILL WINNING INDYCAR RACES INTO THE 1994 SEASON...

car for its new team leader and the necessary sponsorship was duly raised for Emerson's elder brother Wilson to drive for the rival Brabham team.

Wilson Senior, the boys' father, was commentating at this historic meeting and understandably became almost hysterical with vocal pride as his offspring led the pack in 1–2 formation at the end of the opening lap. Sadly for the passionately enthusiastic Paulistas, Emerson spun off and retired with suspension failure, leaving brother Wilson to finish third behind the Argentinian driver, Carlos Reutemann. But the fuse had been

formidable team-mate within the Lotus ranks. This new arrival was Ronnie Peterson, the blond, baby-faced Swede who had been one of Fittipaldi's contemporaries – and close rivals – during their scramble up the ladder in F2 and F3. Ronnie had gained a reputation for enormous skill and car control, but his technical knowledge was minimal. He would come to rely considerably on Emerson's skill when it came to the complex business of setting up the Lotus F1 chassis to best effect.

It quickly dawned on Fittipaldi that this could develop into a no-win situation for him. Peterson had the edge in terms of pure

...A GENERATION AWAY FROM HIS GRAND PRIX DEBUT IN A LOTUS 49 IN THE 1970 BRITISH GRAND PRIX AT BRANDS HATCH.

lit and Brazil would host its first World Championship Grand Prix the following year. The race has remained a firm fixture on the international calendar ever since.

By the time Emerson returned to win the inaugural Brazilian Grand Prix proper at the start of 1973, he was partnered by a new and speed and, with easy access to Emerson's knowledge of what made the Lotus 72 tick, the Brazilian soon found himself in a position where he was doing groundwork which his team-mate could use to beat him. Emerson only won three races that season, Peterson four, but by splitting the success of the Lotus team they allowed Jackie Stewart to win the Drivers' World Championship.

It wasn't quite what Emerson wanted, so he opened negotiations to join the rival McLaren team for 1974. Marlboro, which had spent two years backing the fading British BRM team, made the switch with him to kindle a sponsor/team partnership which lasts to this day. The partnership turned out to be a profitable one. Emerson won three races in 1974 to clinch his second World Championship at the final round with a fourth place in the United States Grand Prix at Watkins Glen.

By this time, Fittipaldi had developed a meticulously precise driving style which he applied to such good effect that his cars almost looked as if they were running on rails. He was gentle on the machinery and,

PUTTING A BRAVE FACE ON IT. AFTER LEAVING McLAREN AT THE END OF 1975, FITTIPALDI HAD A TOUGH TIME WITH HIS OWN F1 TEAM THROUGH TO THE END OF THE DECADE.

by the start of 1975, firmly established as the natural successor to Jackie Stewart at the very pinnacle of F1 achievement. But from then on, he took a series of decisions which would cause his F1 career to steadily unravel.

At the end of that 1975 season, in which he finished runner-up to Niki Lauda in the World Championship, Emerson decided to leave McLaren. He now chose to join the team founded by his brother Wilson with backing from Copersucar, the Brazilian national sugar cartel. Fittipaldi had raced the first Copersucar in 1975 with Wilson driving, but this proved uncompetitive and unreliable. At the end of the season, Wilson retired from driving to concentrate his efforts on supporting

> **BUT FROM THEN ON, HE TOOK A SERIES OF DECISIONS WHICH WOULD CAUSE HIS F1 CAREER TO STEADILY UNRAVEL**

Emerson's career.

The result was a brutally disappointing, protracted and painful decline. Having finished second in the title chase for McLaren in 1975, Emerson found himself 16th in 1976, 12th in 1977 and 9th in 1978. On the face of it, this might appear to indicate a steady improvement in the Copersucar Fittipaldi team's fortunes. In fact, Emerson's 1978 results were boosted dramatically by a glorious, never-to-be-forgotten second place to Carlos Reutemann's Ferrari in the Brazilian Grand Prix at Rio.

Copersucar Fittipaldi had only scored three Championship points in 1976, but worse was to come in 1979 when Emerson slumped to a depressing 21st in the final points table, with just a single point for sixth place in the Argentine GP to his credit. Things perked up a little in 1980, when future champion Keke Rosberg joined the

STARTING THE SEASON WITH A WIN: EMERSON CELEBRATES HIS FIRST VICTORY AS REIGNING WORLD CHAMPION AT THE 1973 ARGENTINE GRAND PRIX.

team, but there was no denying that time was running out for the organization's credibility. Lack of technical expertise and an increasingly severe shortage of cash forced the team to close its doors in 1982.

Emerson had retired from the cockpit prior to the start of the 1981 season, intending to direct the team which carried the family name, his young Brazilian protégé Chico Serra assuming the driving responsibilities together with Rosberg. But his ambitions of becoming a respected F1 team patriarch foundered when Fittipaldi Automotive ceased operations. Emerson may well have achieved a great deal, but he was still only 35 years old. Privately, he knew he had potentially much more to give.

Having moved to North America to explore the possibility of reviving his Indycar career, Emerson returned to the cockpit of a powerful single-seater racing car in 1984 when he made his Indycar debut in the Long Beach street race.

AWAY FROM THE RACE TRACKS, EMERSON HAS BEEN EQUALLY SHREWD WHEN IT COMES TO BUSINESS INVESTMENTS

Driving a March-Cosworth, he qualified 12th and finished 5th. His appetite duly whetted, he now thirsted for a full-time racing return.

In 1985 he joined Patrick Racing and, four years later, won the Indy 500 for the first time at the wheel of the team's Penske-Chevy PC18. The old magic touch had not eluded him. By 1986, his Indycar earnings had topped $1 million before he'd managed his 33rd race start in the category.

In 1990 Fittipaldi joined the front line works Marlboro Penske team, achieving a consistently high level of success – enough to guarantee his enduring place in the team into the 1995 season. By then, Emerson had started 167 Indycar races, winning 21 and starting from pole position on 17 occasions.

He had earned a total of $13,272,873 dollars, placing him second on the career-earnings list, with a lifestyle to match.

Emerson and his wife Teresa now live the millionaire life in Key Biscayne, Florida, with their two children and Emerson's three others from a previous marriage. He commutes to the races – and back to his native Brazil – in his own seven-seat Lear 35A executive jet, the call signs of which is 'EF500,' combining his initials with his most memorable wins in the Indy 500. In the drive of his spacious mansion stand a few vehicles: a Mercedes-Benz 500SL, a Jeep Grand Cherokee, a 1953 Cadillac convertible and a Mercedes S500 saloon.

Away from the race tracks, Emerson has been equally shrewd when it comes to business investments. He has no fewer than 50 franchises for the German Hugo Boss menswear range in Brazil, a 750,000-tree orange grove in his native land and he also markets his own range of Fittipaldi motoring accessories in the USA. He is a consultant for Chrysler/Jeep Eagle and Wellcraft, for whom he designed a high performance boat called the Fittipaldi Scarab.

It seems an age away since the youthful Brazilian with the perpetually mischievous grin stepped off the Varig flight from São Paulo at London's Heathrow airport in the early spring of 1969. Within weeks, he was winning British minor league Formula Ford races. From that day, Emerson Fittipaldi has never looked back.

Few drivers in history have successfully fashioned a second racing career out of the ruins of a first. Yet Emerson Fittipaldi did just that. Even more to the point, at the age of 48, he seems not to have finished just yet. Not by a long way.

AT 48 YEARS OF AGE, EMERSON FITTIPALDI IS STILL COMPETITIVE ON THE US INDYCAR TRAIL – AND HAS ACHIEVED A DEGREE OF BUSINESS SUCCESS, WHICH WAS UNTHINKABLE WHEN HE STARTED OUT IN THE SPORT.

RIGHT: THE FIRST OF LAUDA'S SUCCESSES CAME IN THE SLEEK F1 FERRARI 312B3, SEEN HERE AT MONACO IN 1974. HE DIDN'T WIN THE RACE UNTIL THE FOLLOWING YEAR BUT SCORED TWO VICTORIES DURING THE FIRST OF HIS FOUR SEASONS WITH THE LEGENDARY ITALIAN TEAM.

NIKI LAUDA STILL BEARS THE SCARS OF HIS NEAR-FATAL FIERY ACCIDENT IN THE 1976 GERMAN GRAND PRIX.

The huge Boeing 767 jet liner settles into its final approach to Sydney's Kingsford Smith International airport on the last leg of its two-stop journey from Vienna. Passengers are raising their trays and fumbling with their seat belts as the captain's voice comes over the intercom: "Thank you for flying LaudaAir, and we hope we will have the pleasure of your company again sometime soon."

The usual, briskly efficient protocol of an international airline. Perhaps only a handful of passengers will have noticed the name on the nose of the aircraft — Enzo Ferrari — and even fewer that the clipped Austrian tones from the pilot's seat, which delivered the brief message in such fluent English, were those of triple World Champion racing driver Niki Lauda.

The Austrian ace has packed more into the past 20 years than most people could manage in four lifetimes. He won his first Grand Prix for Ferrari in 1974, took his first Championship the following year and then nearly died in a horrifying accident when his Ferrari crashed in flames during the 1976 German Grand Prix at Nurburgring. He has admitted that the sight of a priest arriving to offer him the Last Rites of the Catholic Church gave him such a terrible shock that he mentally galvanized himself into a near-immediate recovery.

He suffered scorched lungs from inhaling the toxic fumes that eminated from his wrecked Ferrari's burning reinforced plastic bodywork, but Lauda forced the pace of his rehabilitation to such incredible effect that he was back behind the wheel — finishing fourth in the Italian Grand Prix — barely two short months after his brush with death. The accident left him with serious facial burns, which he carries to this day, but he went on to regain the Championship in 1977. He went into retirement two years later to concentrate on his fledgling airline. Lauda then returned to F1 with McLaren in 1982 to win his third Championship two years later before retiring for good at the end of 1985.

There was nothing in his childhood that pointed towards such a brilliant motor racing career. The scion of a wealthy Viennese family with banking and paper processing interests, Niki learned to drive at the wheel of an elderly Volkswagen purchased by his parents in 1949, the year of their son's birth. Photographs of the young buck-toothed lad dressed up in traditional Austrian garb as a schoolboy reveal a child who, by his own

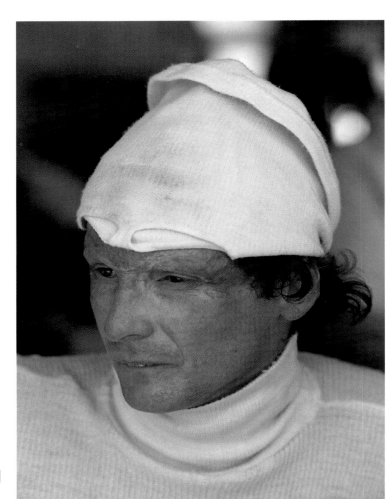

admission, looked a bit of a drip. Certainly, there was no visible indication that he would scale any great mountains of achievement during his lifetime!

With good cause, you could say that Niki Lauda has been a high-stakes gambler from the very start of his racing career. In 1971 he borrowed £8,500 from an Austrian bank to fund his entry into international Formula 2 racing with the British March team. From the very start, he demonstrated a smooth, precise driving style, but this was still not sufficiently successful for the scope of his future talent to appear obvious.

For the 1972 season, Niki was determined to sustain the momentum of his flickering career, such as it was. Towards the end of 1971, he signed a contract to pay the March team a total of £32,000 for the privilege of

driving in both F2 and Grands Prix. At the time, this was regarded as an enormous sum of money. Most observers believed that Niki had taken complete leave of his senses. But that was not the full extent of his eventual financial gamble!

Niki's grandfather, who he always called 'Old Lauda', heard about the sponsorship deal on Vienna's financial grapevine and promptly intervened to have his grandson's deal withdrawn. By then, however, Niki had signed the deal with March. Come what may, he had to find the finances. So he went to another Austrian bank – the Raiffeisenkasse – and negotiated a complex package whereby he borrowed the money in return for an insurance policy for the same value on his own life! It seemed like total insanity on the part of the young Austrian, and even more so

NIKI WAS A GREAT PAL AND CONTEMPORARY OF BRITISH STAR JAMES HUNT THROUGHOUT THE 1970S...

when the 1972 March F1 car proved to be an absolute uncompetitive pup. Although he continued to do well in F2, Niki finished the season with nothing on his Grand Prix scorecard – and he still had to pay back £32,000 to the enterprising bank!

Unshakably confident in his own ability – and buttressed by the knowledge that he had always been just as quick as his team-mate, the highly regarded Ronnie Peterson, during testing – Niki managed to get a deal together to join the British BRM team for 1973. This was a complicated bargain whereby he would contribute financial sponsorship in exchange for the drive – although, in reality, Niki was relying on earning sufficient income from prize money in F1 with BRM, and Touring Car races for BMW, to meet his obligations.

He drove well enough, but eventually had to come clean and advise the BRM team chief, the elderly Louis Stanley (who had married into the same family of wealthy industrialists that had bankrolled the British team since the early 1950s), that he couldn't meet his final payment. Fine, said Stanley, we will waive the final payment in exchange for a contract until the end of 1975. Niki, knowing he had no choice, duly put his signature to the agreement.

Privately, however, Lauda had other ideas. He had been approached by Ferrari with an offer for 1974 and, BRM commitment notwithstanding, he knew he had no choice but to accept. Rightly judging that BRM was a fading force in F1, he accepted Ferrari's invitation only to find himself inevitably embroiled with Stanley in some complicated legal juggling. The matter was eventually

...AND A DECADE LATER STRUCK UP A SIMILAR PROFESSIONAL RELATIONSHIP WITH THE DYNAMIC ALAIN PROST WHEN THEY WERE TEAM-MATES IN THE McLAREN LINE-UP.

resolved when Niki proved that BRM owed him some money which had never been paid.

Lauda arrived at Ferrari just as the well-known Maranello team was poised for an upsurge in performance, under the organizational instigation of Luca di Montezemolo, today the company's President. Armed with the splendid 312B3 chassis, Niki went on to win two races during his maiden season with the team. Then, for 1975, chief engineer Mauro Forghieri penned the very splendid Ferrari 312T and this carried Niki to his first Championship title with a total of five more race wins.

At the start of 1976, Niki seemed set to continue winning, opening the new season by being first past the chequered flag in both the Brazilian and South African Grands Prix. But it soon became clear that he would have to contend with a progressively strengthening challenge from his old friend James Hunt, who had joined the McLaren team as the successor to Emerson Fittipaldi.

His personal life had also moved on. In late 1975 he split with his longtime girlfriend Mariella Reininghaus, heiress to an Austrian brewery fortune, and fell head-over-heels for

Marlene Knaus, a former girlfriend of the actor Curt Jurgens. They married in the spring of 1976 and remain together today, despite an oft-stormy relationship. "When I married Marlene, the first things I lost were all my sweaters, the second thing my Range Rover", he recounts, as if to set the scene of their slightly off-beat partnership in an appropriate perspective.

By the time he crashed in the German Grand Prix, Niki was leading the World Championship contest by the margin of 58 points to James's 35. But as Niki was being transported away to hospital in Cologne, James led the restarted German race from start to finish. The Englishman then went on to finish fourth in Austria and win again in Holland, before Niki returned to finish fourth at Monza. They finished the Italian event with Lauda still ahead of Hunt, but with the gap down to 61-56.

However, Hunt would subsequently find himself disqualified retrospectively from his precious victory over Lauda in the British Grand Prix for an apparent infringement of the rules. This meant that the duo went into the final three races of the season with Niki

on 64 points and James on 47. It still seemed as though Lauda would be able to scrape home and retain his title.

As history now relates, Niki withdrew from the rain-soaked Japanese Grand Prix, unwilling to risk his neck on a near-flooded track. Hunt, despite a late pit stop to change a deflated tyre, would finish third behind Mario Andretti's Lotus and Patrick Depailler's Tyrrell. It was enough to give the Englishman the World Championship by a single point. With characteristic candour, Lauda refused to make excuses for his withdrawal, despite efforts on the part of the Ferrari management to conceal the true reason behind his retirement from this crucial race. The emotional Italian sporting press tore him to shreds, saying he was finished, washed-up and had no future in F1. To compound Niki's personal pain, the Ferrari team signed up Carlos Reutemann as his team-mate for 1977. Lauda couldn't stand him and vowed to get even in the most convincing manner possible – by beating him on the track.

Niki successfully regained his World Championship in 1977 – then quit Ferrari to join the emergent Brabham-Alfa Romeo team. This was run by British entrepreneur Bernie Ecclestone, the man who would, over the following decade, develop Grand Prix racing into a high profile, multi-million dollar globally televised sport. Niki won two races in 1978, then abruptly told Ecclestone – midway through practice for the 1979 Canadian Grand Prix – that he wanted to retire. He left the circuit immediately and, within a day, was in California discussing the delivery details of a new DC-10 airliner to his fledgling airline, LaudaAir.

HE WILL ALWAYS BE REMEMBERED AS ONE OF THE MOST PRAGMATIC, LOGICAL GRAND PRIX DRIVERS OF ALL TIME...

For more than two years, Niki absented himself from the Grand Prix circuits of the world. Yet he continued to harbour the nagging suspicion that he had retired too soon. At the end of 1981, he decided to return to racing and did a deal with the Marlboro McLaren team for the following season. A clause in his contract provided for McLaren to dispose of his services after four races if he didn't prove sufficiently competitive. But he won his third Grand Prix with the team and his future was secured.

He added another victory to his tally of successes in 1982, failed to win a single race the following year, but then bounced back dramatically in 1984 when McLaren came out with its dramatic new Porsche-made TAG turbo engine. Partnered by the young French rising star Alain Prost, the McLaren teamsters won 12 of the season's 16 races, Prost taking seven victories to Lauda's five. But Niki wound up clinching his third title by the wafer-thin margin of half a point from the Frenchman at the final race of the year.

At the end of 1985, having won the 25th victory of his illustrious career in that season's Dutch Grand Prix, Niki Lauda finally made the decision to retire for good. He will always be remembered as one of the most pragmatic, logical Grand Prix drivers of all time, with an intelligently strategic approach to his chosen sport. Blessed with a meticulously tidy and consistent driving style, he always did just enough to secure the result he needed and seldom subjected himself to risks he deemed unrealistic.

Since then, he has built LaudaAir into a formidable force on the international aviation scene, to the point where the German national carrier, Lufthansa, now has a significant stake in his company. In 1992, he also took on the role of consultant to the Ferrari F1 team. Niki himself is qualified to fly his airline's Boeing 767s – the other three

LAUDA EN ROUTE TO HIS FINAL
GRAND PRIX VICTORY IN
HOLLAND, 1985. HE RETIRED
FOR GOOD AT THE END OF THE
SEASON TO CONCENTRATE ON HIS
FLOURISHING AIRLINE BUSINESS.

ON THE VICTORY ROSTRUM AT
ESTORIL AFTER THE 1984
PORTUGUESE GRAND PRIX.
LAUDA FINISHED SECOND TO
PROST, BUT CLAIMED THE TITLE
BY THE UNPRECEDENTED NARROW
MARGIN OF HALF A POINT.

of which are named *Johann Strauss*, *James
Dean* and *Franz Schubert* – as well as the
four smaller 737s named *Janis Joplin*, *Bob
Marley*, *Elvis Presley* and *John Lennon*,
reflecting the owner's somewhat eclectic
musical tastes!

In the spring of 1992, some 16 years after
looking death in the face after his accident at
Nurburgring, Niki Lauda was forced to face
tragedy again, this time on a vastly more
horrifying scale. A LaudaAir Boeing 767, en
route from Bangkok to Vienna, broke up in
flight over Thailand with the loss of all
aboard. Niki immediately flew to the jungle
crash site, reasoning that it was crucially
important for the airline chief to be present
on the spot at such a moment of disaster.

The strength of character, and efforts to
hide his own personal grief at the loss of
colleagues who were close personal friends,
in the face of a relentless international
television spotlight, offered an even more
profound insight into Niki Lauda's personal
courage than any of his achievements on the
race tracks of the world.

RIGHT: CAPTAIN LAUDA – THE
MAN WHO SWAPPED THE COCKPIT
OF A McLAREN FOR A BOEING
767!

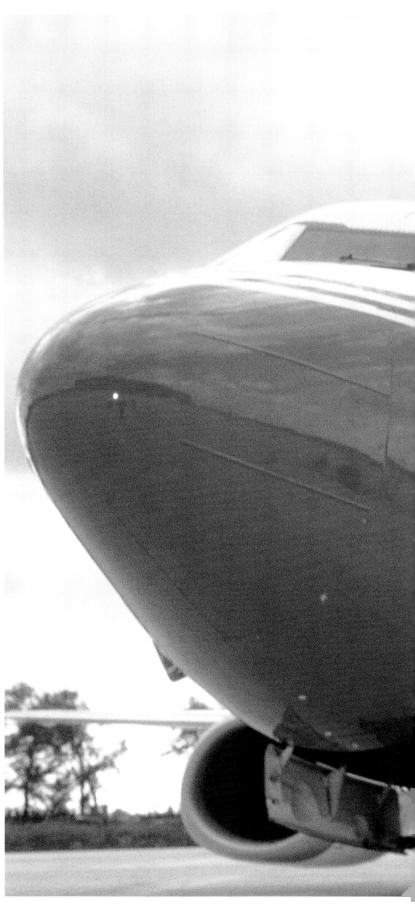

RIGHT: THE ABSOLUTE ZENITH OF
HUNT'S ACHIEVEMENT CAME IN
1976, AT THE WHEEL OF THE
MCLAREN, WHEN HE WON THE
WORLD CHAMPIONSHIP BY A
SINGLE POINT FROM HIS CLOSE
FRIEND NIKI LAUDA. HERE HE
LEADS JODY SCHECKTER'S
TYRELL DURING THAT YEAR'S
LONG BEACH GRAND PRIX, A
WEEKEND ON WHICH THE NEWS
BROKE THAT HIS WIFE SUSY HAD
LEFT HIM FOR RICHARD BURTON.

DOING THE RIGHT THING: JAMES
PUTS ON A SMILE FOR A TEXACO
HAVOLINE OIL COMMERCIAL.

J ames Hunt's extrovert, devil-may-care
lifestyle may well have served as a
touchstone for his times, but it often
served to conceal just how seriously this
public school-educated Englishman took his
professional motor racing career. Hunt won
the World Championship but once, in 1976,
following a battle against the mathematical
odds, and retired from the cockpit in the
middle of the 1979 season after suddenly
concluding that the risks didn't make much
sense any longer.

That he would die in bed of a heart attack
at the age of 45, long after he had exchanged
the risks of the race track for less frenetic
pursuits, seemed doubly ironic. In his early
motor racing career, James quickly inherited
the soubriquet 'Hunt the Shunt' and there
were times when it seemed questionable
whether his driving style would allow him to
survive a career in this most potentially
hazardous of sports.

Despite those early disappointments and
setbacks, there was always something about
Hunt that suggested he would make the Big
Time, if only he caught the right car at the
right time. His progress in Formula 3 was
spectacular and erratic, but always very fast.
Of course, the truth was that he frequently
found himself saddled with an uncompetitive
car – usually a March – and it was only
thanks to the support of Lord Hesketh, who
became his patron, that he was able to obtain
a year-old March F2 car to contest a limited
programme of races towards the end of the
1972 season.

That marked the turning point. Thomas
Alexander Fermor-Hesketh was a true British
Blue Blood, but in many ways an obvious
soul mate to Hunt, whose burgeoning racing
career he would now support. Educated at
Ampleforth, he was reputed to have made a
fortune well in excess of £1 million buying
and selling a Scottish estate when he was
barely 20 years old.

This allowed him to finance his motor
racing ambitions, which would see James
propelled into the Grand Prix front line
during 1973: first at the wheel of a privately
entered March, later with his Lordship's
specially designed machine, the Hesketh 308.

The team operated out of the stable block
at Easton Neston, the 18th-century manor
set in 5,000 acres of Northamptonshire
countryside near Towcester. It was also just a
three minute helicopter flight from the
paddock at Silverstone, where Hunt scored
his first F1 victory in the 1974 International
Trophy race.

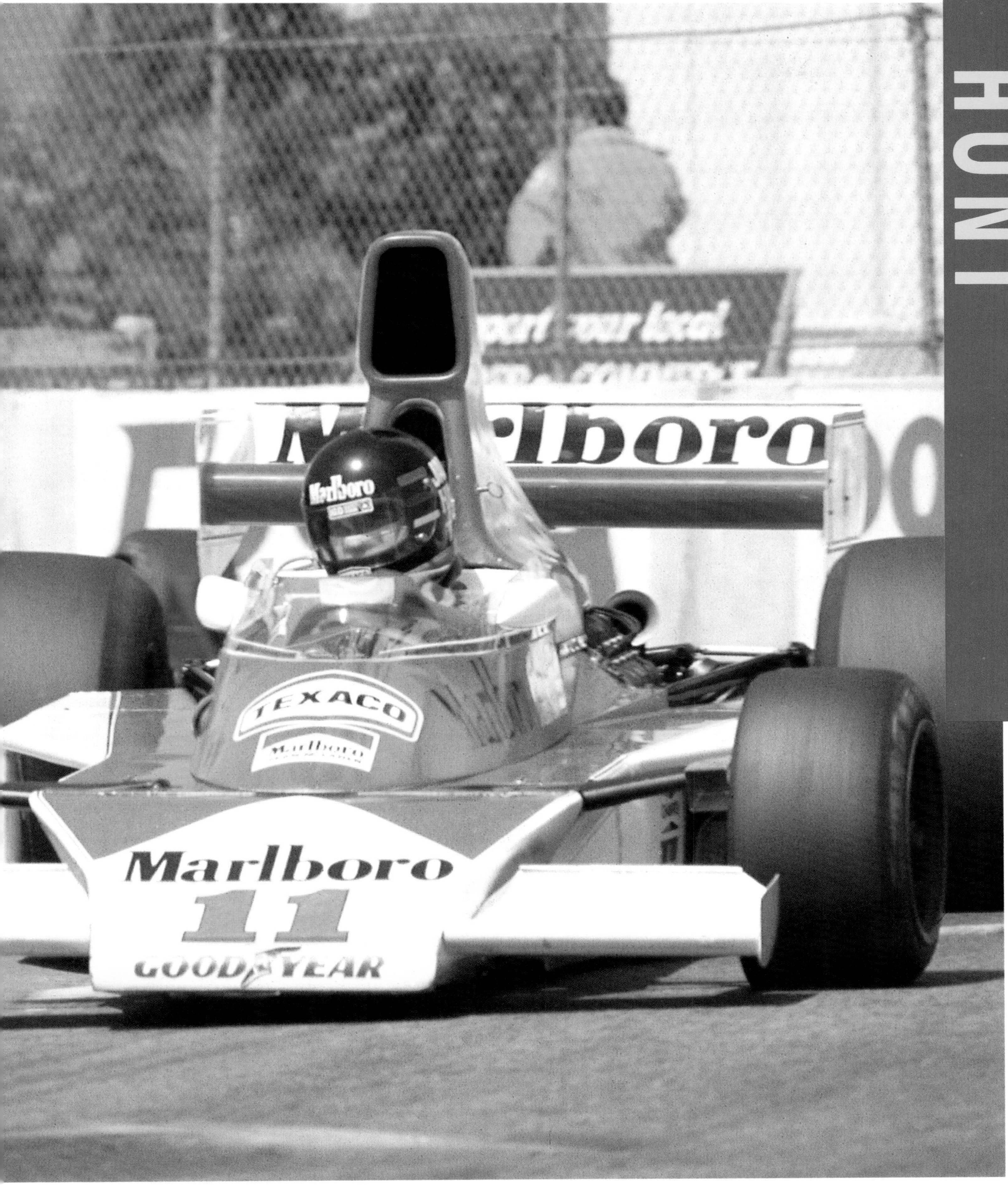
Marlboro
TEXACO
Marlboro
11
GOODYEAR

Off the track, James was a first rate hell-raiser and womanizer, facets of his character which led many people to conclude that he was not very serious about his motor racing. Quite the contrary was in fact the case. His second place in the 1973 United States Grand Prix at Watkins Glen, where his Hesketh March finished just a matter of yards behind Ronnie Peterson's winning Lotus 72, said everything about his serious commitment to professionalism at this early stage of his F1 career.

In June 1975, by which time Hesketh had spent around £500,000 of his fortune on motor racing, Hunt won the Dutch Grand Prix at Zandvoort after a terrific battle with Niki Lauda's Ferrari. By any standards, this success in tricky wet/dry track conditions was a superbly judged performance. Despite this, Alexander decided it was time to shut up shop six months later because he was unable to raise any commercial sponsorship to support his investment, and James suddenly found himself contemplating the unpleasant prospect of unemployment.

However, within weeks, Emerson Fittipaldi

LAID BACK. JAMES HUNT'S RELAXED DEMEANOUR AWAY FROM THE COCKPIT OF A GRAND PRIX CAR BELIED THE EXTREME SERIOUSNESS WITH WHICH HE PURSUED HIS CHOSEN SPORT.

announced that he would be leaving the McLaren squad to join his brother's F1 team, which was backed by Copersucar. It was only a matter of days before McLaren boss Teddy Mayer contacted Hunt and a deal was struck for him to take over the Brazilian's position in the famous British team. James would be paid £40,000 for his services in 1976 – but would renew his deal for £200,000 the next year after winning the Championship in his first season with McLaren.

Armed with the formidable McLaren M23, Hunt immediately established himself as team leader by qualifying fastest in practice for the Brazilian Grand Prix, his first race of the new season. But he would be dogged by a succession of setbacks during the course of the season as the McLaren team was called to account for various rule infringements.

After winning the Spanish Grand Prix at Madrid's Jarama circuit, where he beat Niki Lauda into second place, Hunt's McLaren was deemed to have infringed the maximum rear-track dimensions and was disqualified. McLaren appealed and the win was later restored to them. But it was at Brands Hatch, in front of his passionately supportive home crowd, that James would suffer the cruellest disappointment of the year.

His McLaren was involved in a multiple collision on the first corner, and the race was red-flagged to a halt and started again. The rules at the time stated that anybody whose car was not still running when the red flag was shown at the start/finish line would not be permitted to take the restart. There was considerable controversy over whether or not this was the case as far as Hunt was concerned. After endless deliberation, the stewards permitted him to take the restart, his damaged car by now having been fully repaired.

Thereafter, James provided the crowd with just what they'd paid to see. Niki Lauda made

the initial running, but James steadily reeled him in, overtaking the Ferrari in a truly audacious manoeuvre – under-braking for the tricky Druids hairpin – and storming away to win the race. Ferrari lodged an appeal against Hunt being permitted to take the restart and, three months later, James experienced a sense of crushing anti-climax when the victory was annulled.

Of course, for the British tabloid press, James's antics represented meat and drink, both for the sports and social editors. Here was this blond, tousle-haired hero going into battle against the wretched Foreigner in a season when he lost out in love: his first wife Susy had sought solace elsewhere, in the arms of Richard Burton. The media simply lapped it up!

Yet all this controversy merely served to strengthen Hunt's resolve. He went on to win the German, Dutch, Canadian and United States Grands Prix to bring himself within striking distance of Lauda's points total as they both went into that final race in the torrential rain at Japan's Mount Fuji circuit.

James displayed superhuman levels of concentration and commitment on that dank afternoon when standing water lay inches deep on the track surface. He took an immediate lead and totally dominated the event until his McLaren sustained a punctured tyre in the closing stages.

James was almost quivering with thinly-suppressed fury as he struggled into the pit lane. It seemed to take absolute ages for the mechanics to jack up the McLaren in order to fit a fresh front wheel and tyre. Then he went back into the race in sixth place, going like a rocket and thereafter passing each and every

JAMES DISPLAYED SUPERHUMAN LEVELS OF CONCENTRATION AND COMMITMENT ON THAT DANK AFTERNOON WHEN STANDING WATER LAY INCHES DEEP ON THE TRACK SURFACE

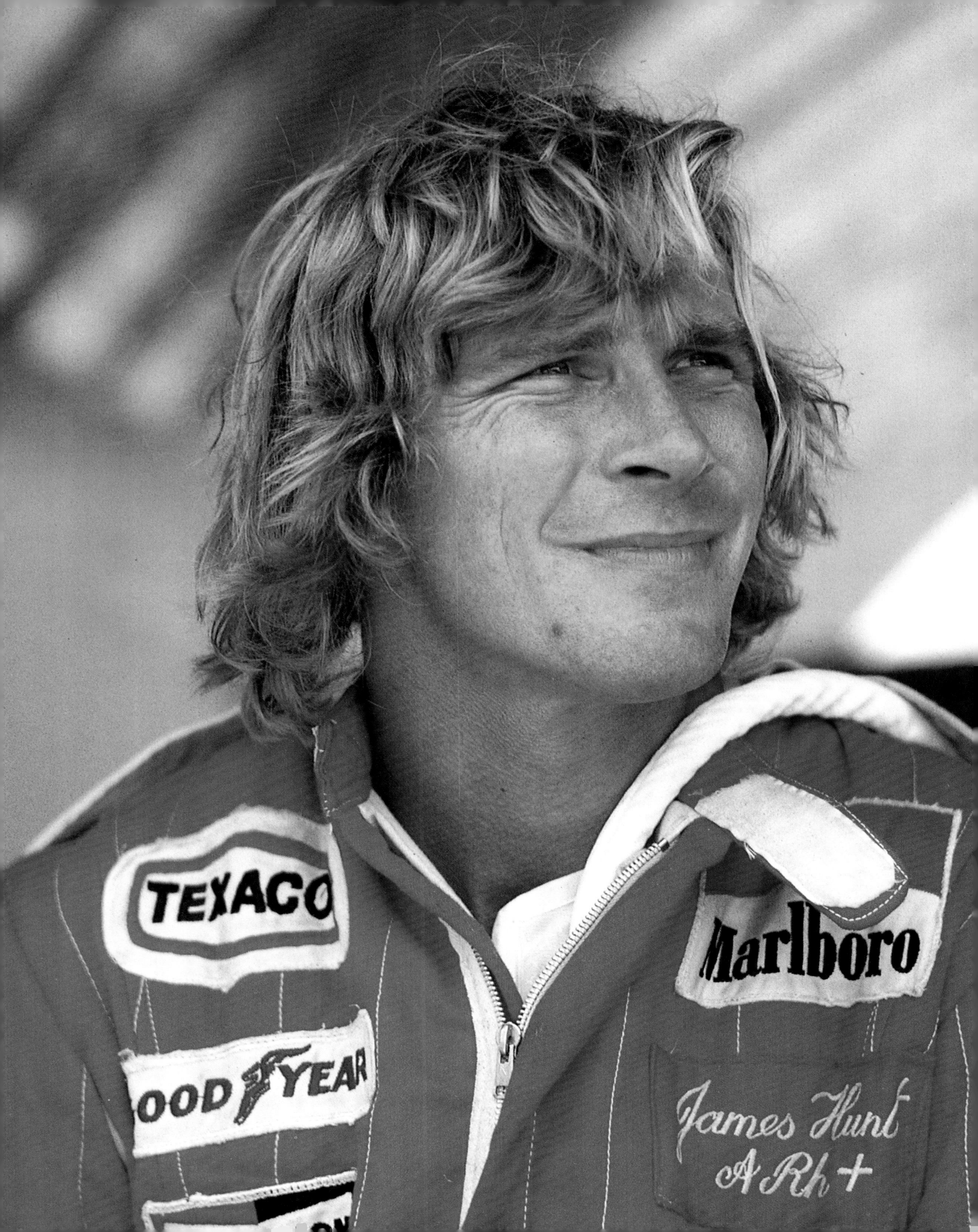
TEXACO
Marlboro
OODYEAR
James Hunt
A Rh +

LEFT: THE TOUSLE-HAIRED HUNT CARED LITTLE FOR THE ACCEPTED CONVENTIONS WHEN IT CAME TO DEALING WITH SPONSORS. HE CARRIED THE McLAREN TEAM'S MARLBORO AND TEXACO SPONSORSHIP ON HIS OVERALLS, BUT WAS ALWAYS A MAVERICK WHEN IT CAME TO HIS OFF-TRACK DRESS CODE.

car the second he came upon it.

As Mario Andretti's Lotus 77 sped past the chequered flag to take the win from Patrick Depailler's Tyrrell P34 six-wheeler, Hunt slammed past the chequered flag, inwardly uncertain of where he was in the final order. Back in the pit lane, he erupted from the cockpit and was well into delivering a verbal tongue-lashing to the hapless McLaren crew before team manager Teddy Mayer could interrupt to say; "James, you were *third*. You are World Champion!"

The performance he gave in that final and crucial race of the season was an absolutely representative reflection of his talent as a racing driver. Once the race was underway, he could be an inspired performer, but in the immediate prelude to the start he was always buttoned up with nerves. Often he became so agitated he was physically sick, a dramatic counterpoint to his friend and rival Niki Lauda who always seemed to be cool, calm and mentally extremely well organized.

> **ONCE THE RACE WAS UNDERWAY, HE COULD BE AN INSPIRED PERFORMER, BUT IN THE IMMEDIATE PRELUDE TO THE START HE WAS ALWAYS BUTTONED UP WITH NERVES**

As the reigning World Champion, Hunt continued to drive well through into the 1977 season, despite the fact that the McLaren team's technical edge was steadily being eroded by its key rivals: Lotus, Ferrari, Wolf and Brabham. James would go on to win three Grands Prix that season, including an uncontroversial and well-merited success in the British race at Silverstone, plus the US race at Watkins Glen and the Japanese race, again at Mount Fuji, but this time long after the Championship had been regained by Lauda.

In 1978 McLaren's form dipped quite alarmingly as Lotus's dramatic ground effect type 79 proved easily the quickest car around, matched occasionally by the mechanically bullet-proof Ferraris. James had been fifth in the 1977 World Championship, but faded to eighth in the 1978 contest and decided to leave McLaren at the end of the season.

In 1979 he joined Walter Wolf's independent F1 team to drive its new WR7 challenger, which had been designed by Harvey Postlethwaite, the man responsible for the Hesketh 308 – the car that had carried Hunt to his joyous first victory in Holland four years earlier.

JAMES ON THE VICTORY ROSTRUM IN THE COMPANY OF MARIO ANDRETTI (LEFT) AFTER WINNING THE 1976 CANADIAN GRAND PRIX AT MOSPORT PARK. THIS WAS A CRUCIAL SUCCESS IN HIS LATE-SEASON CHARGE TOWARDS THE CHAMPIONSHIP TITLE.

For his many fans, it was depressing to watch James Hunt's fall from the high wire in 1978 and early 1979. By his own admission, he was unable to get the best out of an uncompetitive car, which was precisely what the McLaren M26 and the Wolf WR9 had become. With that in mind, there were many people who admired the way in which James took his final decision to quit, even though it meant letting his team down midway through the 1979 season. But he would have done his colleagues more of a disservice had he continued without the proper motivation.

For the last 14 years of his life, James Hunt became one of motor racing's most informed television commentators and his double act with Murray Walker made BBC's coverage of the World Championship one of the most popular shows on the British screen. James was totally honest; there was nothing he said about any driver on the air that he wouldn't have said to the man's face. By the same token, he was unstinting in his praise of others, be they drivers or even journalists, many of whom he would often ring up out of the blue just to catch up on the latest gossip.

Only after James's sudden death did the motor racing community come to hear of

the inner mental anguish which inexplicably tormented this enormously popular man. Despite financial worries stemming from various business setbacks, as well as a costly divorce from his second wife Sarah – the mother of his two sons Freddie and Tom – he had always been a consistently hospitable host at his beautiful Wimbledon home.

In 1990, he briefly toyed with a Grand Prix comeback, testing a Williams-Renault at the Paul Ricard circuit in southern France. He saw this as a possible means of restoring his personal motivation – not to mention his depleted finances. He was not quick enough and, even though he privately believed he could get back into competitive trim, the idea never came to anything. But he stayed closely involved on the professional racing scene, advising and tutoring a number of up-and-coming drivers including current McLaren-Mercedes star Mika Hakkinen.

Overwhelmingly, James Hunt will be remembered as a fine racing driver and a kindly person. But he had lived his personal life in the fast lane for more than 20 years, with more drinking, smoking and dope-taking than was good for him. The motor racing community misses him still.

HUNT'S GREATEST DAY? ON THE ROSTRUM AFTER WINNING THE 1977 BRITISH GRAND PRIX AT SILVERSTONE AHEAD OF NIKI LAUDA (RIGHT) AND THE SWEDISH DRIVER GUNNAR NILSSON (LEFT).

HUNT CARRIED THE COLOURS OF HIS OLD SCHOOL, WELLINGTON COLLEGE, ON HIS HELMET THROUGHOUT HIS RACING CAREER.

Mario
ANDRETTI
1978

The scene is an Indycar race at Portland, Oregon. The date is 15 June, 1986. On the final lap of the race, Michael Andretti's blue and yellow March comes out of the last corner and begins to accelerate towards the chequered flag. Suddenly, the car slows down, misfiring as its engine struggles to pick up the last few drops of fuel in its tank.

Slowing down all the time, Michael limps towards the chequered flag. Suddenly, a red Lola storms out of the final turn, roars up the start/finish straight and just pips him at the post by less than a second. Its driver?

Michael's 46-year-old father Mario Andretti, one of the most well-known racing drivers America has ever produced.

After the race, Michael hints to his father that, under the circumstances, it would have been nice if the Old Man had seen fit to throw him the win on this occasion. Mario's eyes narrowed. "That's not the way it works, Michael", he told his son sternly. After all, it was Father's Day.

The story says everything about Mario Gabriele Andretti's fight to rise up through the motor racing ranks. Born near Trieste, Italy in the early months of the Second World War, Mario and his family went to a displaced person's camp. They were to spend the next seven years there, after their native region was incorporated into Yugoslavia and the map of Europe was re-jigged as a result of the Axis defeat.

From his early teens, Mario and his twin brother Aldo were completely capitivated by motor racing. They especially liked following the exploits of Italian legend Alberto Ascari, who won the World Championship for Ferrari in 1952 and 1953. The Andretti youngsters were brought up believing that Italy was the epicentre of the motor racing world. Later, Mario would fondly recount how, at the age of 15, he cycled from the family home near Lucca to watch in hypnotized fascination as the Mercedes-Benz 300SLR, crewed by Stirling Moss and Denis Jenkinson, flashed past en route to victory in the epic 1955 Mille Miglia road race. Less than a month later, the Andretti family decamped for the United States, the twin boys desolated by the thought that they might never see another race in their lives. The Andrettis settled in Nazareth, Pennsylvania, in 1955. Within nine years, Mario would be barnstorming his way round the precarious US dirt tracks, cutting his motor racing teeth.

He first went to Indianapolis in 1965, and

Andre

Valvoline

four years later, Mario went out and won the Memorial Day classic in a back-up car after a fiery practice accident, which left him with distinctive flash burns on both cheeks. Even then, Mario was developing into a tough old boy who knew how to handle himself in a tight corner out on the track.

In the spring of 1968, the international racing world was shattered by the death of the legendary Jim Clark. The passing of the shy young Scottish border farmer who went racing essentially for fun, yet quickly rose to become the greatest Grand Prix driver of his era, marked a watershed in the history of the sport. From then on, spearheaded largely by Jackie Stewart's commercial acumen, Grand Prix racing began the transformation into Big Business.

For Colin Chapman's Lotus team, reeling at the loss of its number one driver, it was time to dig in and rebuild. Graham Hill, father of today's Williams F1 star Damon, boosted Lotus morale in dogged fashion by winning the 1968 Championship. But Hill was already 39, old by Grand Prix standards, and Chapman began to look elsewhere for fresh driving talent.

Mario Andretti, then 28, looked a good bet. He was signed to drive the superb Ford-engined Lotus 49 in the US Grand Prix at Watkins Glen and amazed everybody by qualifying on pole position for this, his F1 debut. Although he failed to finish the race, Chapman signed the compact American to drive in as many Grands Prix for Lotus as his Indycar commitments permitted in 1969.

But it did not turn out to be a successful arrangement: the cars were hampered by persistent unreliability and the experiment was terminated at the end of the season. For the time being, at least.

In 1970, Andretti drove an uncompetitive March 701 to even less effect, but a switch to Ferrari the following year yielded his first Grand Prix win, albeit a slightly fortunate success, in South Africa. For the next two years he would continue to enjoy guest outings for the famous Italian team. He then concentrated on Indycars for the whole of 1973 before returning for another stab at F1 with the Vel's Parnelli team, part-owned by 1963 Indy 500 winner Parnelli Jones, at the end of 1974.

Andretti's intermittent love affair with F1 continued on an ad hoc basis until the start of 1976 when the Vel's Parnelli team closed its doors. By then, the fortunes of the Lotus F1 team had reached a low ebb and force of circumstance threw Andretti and Chapman together again. Within another two years, Lotus was back on top with Chapman's sensational ground-effect Lotus 79 and Mario achieved another of his life's ambitions by storming to the 1978 World Championship.

For three glorious years, Chapman and Andretti worked together to great effect. But from 1979 Lotus began to lose its competitive edge. Mario stayed on until the end of 1980, then switched to the Alfa Romeo F1 team for another disappointing season before quitting the Grand Prix stage.

Even then, at the age of 42, he was invited back to drive for the Williams team at Long Beach and what amounted to a glorious finale to his F1 career by events at the 1982 Italian Grand Prix at Monza.

It had been a catastrophic season for the famous Italian team. Its number one driver Gilles Villeneuve was killed in practice for the Belgian GP at Zolder, then Frenchman Didier Pironi, practising in the wet for the German race at Hockenheim, suffered multiple leg injuries which ended his racing career.

Ferrari needed a morale booster, and it fell to Andretti to provide it. His return to the

FOR THREE GLORIOUS YEARS, CHAPMAN AND ANDRETTI WORKED TOGETHER TO GREAT EFFECT

COOL AND UNRUFFLED: ANDRETTI DURING THE 1978 SWEDISH GRAND PRIX WEEKEND.

Italian team somehow represented a symbolic homecoming. When his plane touched down at Milan's Malpensa international airport, a huge gaggle of press photographers and fans was waiting on the tarmac. One by one, all the passengers disembarked. No Mario. The media men exchanged quizzical gazes. But a few seconds later, Andretti appeared alone at the top of the aircraft stairs – wearing a baseball cap emblazoned with the distinctive Ferrari emblem, the black Prancing Horse. It was pure theatre and the onlookers went wild with delight!

Mario qualified the powerful Ferrari 126 turbo on pole position at Monza and finished an excellent third in the race. That would

- - - - - - - -

MARIO QUALIFIED THE POWERFUL FERRARI 126 TURBO ON POLE POSITION AT MONZA AND FINISHED AN EXCELLENT THIRD IN THE RACE

- - - - - - - -

have been a magnificent note on which to round off his glittering F1 career, but there was still the inconsequential Cesar's Palace GP at Las Vegas for him to run, an event from which he sadly retired.

Yet there was plenty more motor racing in Mario Andretti. He returned to America, where he would continue to contest the Indycar championship with unremitting gusto for more than another decade. He passionately wanted to win at Indianapolis for a second time, but, despite coming close on several occasions, that final achievement continued to elude him right up to the end of 1994 when he hung up his helmet for good. Well, not quite; he still planned to continue sports car racing in a handful of endurance events, still aiming to win the Le Mans 24-hour classic as he forged through his mid-fifties.

ANDRETTI AND PETERSON CELEBRATE THAT LAST SUCCESS IN HOLLAND, WITH NIKI LAUDA (RIGHT), WHO FINISHED THIRD IN HIS BRABHAM-ALFA ROMEO.

THE LAST ANDRETTI-PETERSON 1–2 FINISH CAME IN THE 1978 DUTCH GRAND PRIX AT ZANDVOORT, WHERE THE TWO LOTUS 79S PROVED THE CLASS OF THE FIELD.

MARIO HAS RECENTLY BEEN
JOINED ON THE PROFESSIONAL
RACING SCENE BY HIS ELDEST SON
MICHAEL (RIGHT). HERE FATHER
AND SON WAIT FOR THE RAIN TO
EASE AT DAYTONA IN 1991,
WHERE THEY WERE SHARING A
PORSCHE SPORTS CAR IN THE
24-HOUR ENDURANCE EVENT.

More than anything else, Mario Andretti
brought class and a certain charisma to the
international motor racing scene. With a
trim and compact physique, he was always
immaculately groomed and impeccably
mannered. As his black hair became speckled
with white streaks through his mid-forties, he
would have made an excellent understudy for
Marlon Brando in *The Godfather*. He was a
man who liked to travel through life First
Class and, having suffered such poverty as a
child, appreciated the value of a dollar more
keenly than many of his contemporaries.

Away from the circuits, Mario Andretti
was a shrewd businessman, having risen to
millionaire status even before he won the
Formula 1 World Championship in 1978.
He bought a stake in a firm of Wall Street
stockbrokers in the late 1970s, invested

successfully in real estate and a host of lesser
commercial projects. But it was motor racing
that was the love of his life – first, second
and last. By the end of his Indycar racing
career, he had earned over $11 million in
winnings, having competed in a total of 407
races and scoring 52 wins.

The quintessential professional, Mario
Andretti's blood may have been Italian but
he never regarded himself as anything but
an American – and would always proudly
recall the occasion when US citizenship was
formally conferred upon him. To this day, he
lives in the same house he has occupied since
the late 1960s, although the road – once
called Market Street, believe it or not – was
renamed Victory Lane in recognition of his
1969 Indy 500 win. It is difficult to imagine
anything pleasing Mario more.

AFTER THE END OF HIS F1 CAREER
IN 1992, ANDRETTI CONTINUED
WITH INDYCAR RACING IN THE US.
SIXTEEN YEARS AFTER HIS WORLD
CHAMPIONSHIP SUCCESS, ONLY A
FEW MORE GREY HAIRS TO TESTIFY
THE PASSING OF TIME.

Jody SCHECKTER 1979

In many ways, this curly-haired South African is not the first image that springs to mind when tallying up Grand Prix racing's millionaire elite. Having completely severed his links with the sport when he retired from driving, aged 30, at the end of the 1980 season, it is all too easy to forget that the rough, tough South African from East London was regarded as the most dazzling young Formula 1 star when he burst onto the World Championship scene at the wheel of a McLaren-Ford in 1972.

Scheckter credits his father for sparking his interest in motor racing. He owned a couple of garages and encouraged his son to take up karting while in his teens. After his schooling, Jody served an engineering apprenticeship at one of the family garages and began racing seriously in a beaten-up old Renault R8 saloon almost the moment he reached his 18th birthday.

Having cut his teeth in spectacular fashion with this well-worn machine, he switched to the Formula Ford international category. He won the prestigious South African 'Driver to Europe' award – receiving a cheque for 1,000 rands and air tickets to London for him and a friend at the start of 1971. He quickly acquired a racing car with quite a pedigree – a Merlyn Mk11A Formula Ford, which had been used two years earlier by another future World Champion, Emerson Fittipaldi. And, from the moment Scheckter took to the British tracks, he displayed almost instantly the same sort of natural flair and car control which had characterized the Merlyn's former owner.

Jody roared through Formula Ford in a matter of months. Then it was onto the next rung of the ladder – Formula 3. By the start of 1972, he had graduated into the European F2 Championship, which is an intensely competitive category regarded as the holding area for future Grand Prix talent. By the middle of 1972, barely 18 months since stepping off the plane from Johannesburg, Scheckter considered himself ready for the jump to Formula 1.

He was driving for McLaren in F2 and, by contract, they had the first option on his services for Formula 1. When Lotus boss Colin Chapman made an approach to Scheckter, McLaren management became quite indignant about the whole affair, forcefully reminding Jody that his first commitment was legally and morally to them. He declined the Lotus offer, but it had achieved the desired effect. McLaren decided

WINNING THE 1977 ARGENTINE GRAND PRIX, FIRST TIME OUT IN THE NEW WOLF-FORD FIELDED BY THE TEAM THAT BELONGED TO ENTHUSIASTIC AUSTRO-CANADIAN OIL MAGNATE WALTER WOLF.

that he would drive a third car, alongside regular drivers Peter Revson and Denny Hulme, in the 1972 United States Grand Prix at Watkins Glen.

Jody impressed everybody by qualifying his McLaren M19 eighth out of 31 starters. He ran third from the start, but later had a spin which dropped him to an eventual ninth at the chequered flag. He then went on to qualify third to make the front row of the grid in the following year's South African GP, and he led the French race before tangling with Emerson Fittipaldi's Lotus. Then came the 1973 British Grand Prix at Silverstone.

By this stage in his career, Scheckter was going through a potentially hazardous transitional stage, which is always a feature of a really great driver's learning curve. Put simply, his outstanding natural car control was not tempered in any way by a sense of

fear or caution. Trying to make up places too quickly on the opening lap of the Silverstone race, he ran wide coming out of the high speed Woodcote corner, slithered onto the grass – and then came spearing back across the track to collide with the pit wall.

The pack scattered in all directions as the wayward McLaren triggered a multiple pile-up of cataclysmic proportions. Nine cars were badly damaged, the race was flagged to a halt and later restarted. Without Scheckter.

For 1974, Jody moved to Tyrrell, taking over the seat vacated by Jackie Stewart on his retirement. The original plan was for him to partner François Cevert, the debonair French driver who had been tutored by Stewart over three seasons for a future team leadership role. But it was a partnership that never came about. Practising for the final race of 1973, the United States GP, Cevert was killed in a

BEFORE JOINING TYRELL, JODY HAD DRIVEN A HANDFUL OF RACES FOR THE MCLAREN TEAM IN 1972 AND 1973. THE ORANGE BAND ON HIS HELMET MATCHED THE MCLAREN TEAM COLOURS – AND, SENTIMENTALLY, HE RETAINED IT TO THE END OF HIS ACTIVE RACING CAREER.

violent accident at Watkins Glen. The thread of continuity, so crucial for the sustained success of an F1 team, had thus been broken and Scheckter faced the new season partnered by the inexperienced Frenchman Patrick Depailler.

Jody managed to moderate his fiery on-track temperament and wound up winning two races in 1974: the British and Swedish Grands Prix. He stayed on with Tyrrell for the next two seasons, scoring an emotional triumph in front of his home crowd at Kyalami in 1975 and winning again in Sweden the following year. But it was fast becoming clear that a World Championship was unlikely to come his way as long as he stayed with Tyrrell. So he took a gamble for 1977 and signed on for the newly revamped team established by Austro-Canadian oil millionaire Walter Wolf.

In retrospect, it was an inspired decision to seek fresh pastures. Scheckter won three races, including a first-time-out success in the Argentine GP at Buenos Aires. He finished second in the World Championship behind Niki Lauda and stayed with the team through to the end of 1978, though he failed to win another race.

Then came the invitation to join the famous Ferrari squad. Jody, by now living in Monaco, had no doubts in his own mind that he was ready to win a World Championship. Sure enough, his earlier rowdy driving style had become tempered with experience, but he retained all of his original speed. Yet, from the touchlines, many observers predicted it would be a Marriage Made in Hell. Jody had a reputation of being a trifle surly under pressure and the thought of his working with a bunch of excitable Latin Ferrari mechanics seemed destined to end in disarray.

More to the point though, Scheckter found himself driving alongside the French Canadian star Gilles Villeneuve, one of the fastest and least inhibited drivers in post-war motor racing history. In a straight fight, surely Villeneuve would take him to the cleaners? Perhaps in terms of sheer speed, but Jody vowed to be more consistent. He quickly identified that Gilles had the very same lack of inhibition which had been such a factor during his own early racing career.

Now in Monaco, Scheckter became a close neighbour to his team-mate. At first, it was somehow difficult to see what they had in common. But Scheckter and Villeneuve quickly became very close friends, sharing a mutual professional admiration for each other in addition to a very similar sense of humour and appreciation of the absurd.

The pressure was on Jody from the outset, with Villeneuve winning two of the first four races on the Championship calendar. But Scheckter kept his nerve and sustained his consistency, winning the Belgian, Monaco and Italian Grands Prix to clinch the title. In the Monza race, Villeneuve followed dutifully in his wheeltracks, scrupulously abiding by standing team orders not to overtake his rival, even though he knew that Scheckter's car was all that stood between him and the World Championship. As it was, Jody crossed the line first — and clinched the title.

SURE ENOUGH, HIS EARLIER ROWDY DRIVING STYLE HAD BECOME TEMPERED WITH EXPERIENCE, BUT HE RETAINED ALL OF HIS ORIGINAL SPEED

Thereafter, the fire of Scheckter's ambition quickly dimmed. Ferrari was hopelessly uncompetitive in 1980 and Jody decided to retire at the end of the season. He made his decision public in the middle of the year, but loyally fulfilled his obligation to the team right to the final afternoon of his last race.

Among those very sorry to see him go were the Ferrari mechanics. They quickly came to admire his philosophical, slightly

world-weary attitude. Contrary to those early predictions, he slipped easily into the Ferrari team environment and felt instantly at ease in its surroundings.

He left motor racing, but not empty-handed. Scheckter had been paid quite handsomely for two season's work with the team, and very shrewdly negotiated a deal whereby he sold advertising rights to his helmet and overalls to the makers of Brooklyn chewing gum – reputedly for a figure in excess of $1 million.

> CONTRARY TO THOSE EARLY PREDICTIONS, HE SLIPPED EASILY INTO THE FERRARI TEAM ENVIRONMENT AND FELT INSTANTLY AT EASE IN ITS SURROUNDINGS

He had also invested his earnings wisely during his racing career and, although his marriage to Pam – his childhood sweetheart – broke up after he quit driving, Jody made a new life for himself in North America. Now based near Atlanta, Georgia, he founded a company called Firearms Training Systems, which specializes in high-technology security systems and courses in firearms for police and security services. By all accounts, it has proved every bit as successful for Scheckter as did his professional F1 racing career.

SCHECKTER IN THE FUNCTIONAL FERRARI 312T4 EN ROUTE TO SUCCESS IN THE 1979 MONACO GRAND PRIX, ONE OUT OF THE THREE WINS OF THE SEASON THAT TOOK HIM TO THE 1979 TITLE.

RECEIVING HIS TROPHY FROM PRINCESS GRACE AFTER WINNING THAT 1979 MONACO GP.

Alan JONES 1980

RIGHT: ALAN JONES'S MAIDEN F1 SUCCESS CAME IN THE 1977 AUSTRIAN GRAND PRIX AT OSTERREICHRING, WHERE HE SCORED A LUCKY WIN IN THIS SHADOW-FORD DN8.

ALAN JONES WITH THE ENIGMATIC ARGENTINE DRIVER CARLOS REUTEMANN (RIGHT), WHO WAS HIS TEAM-MATE AT WILLIAMS IN 1980 AND 1981. THEY HAD A TENSE PERSONAL RELATIONSHIP, DESPITE THEIR MUTUAL PROFESSIONAL RESPECT.

The image of the modern Grand Prix driver as an athletic, clean-living, early-to-bed professional may have sat just a little precariously on Alan Jones's shoulders. This hard-driving Australian lived his life with gusto, like his father before him. Yet this should not be taken to suggest that the rugged Jones took his Formula 1 driving anything less than seriously. He was one formidable competitor, blending raw bravery and unwavering confidence into a highly motivated cocktail which carried him all the way to the World Championship in 1980.

Like Andretti, Jones was no stranger to hard times. But in Alan's case, it hadn't been simply a question of clawing himself up from nowhere, but a question of watching his family's early wealth being dissipated on the harsh rocks of economic reality. His father, Stan Jones, was a hard-driving, hard-drinking product of Australia's immediate post-war racing era.

Many believe Jones senior was as good – if not better – than his compatriot Jack Brabham who went on to win three World Championships. But when Brabham set off to make his reputation in Europe, Stan stayed in Australia to look after his businesses and to race in domestic national events. However, Stan Jones's business acumen proved less effective. His garage business was decimated in the Australian credit squeeze of the mid-1960s and he went bust.

Born in Melbourne, Alan Jones came to Europe in 1970 at the age of 24 to make a name for himself in Formula 3. He wasn't the most obviously talented member of his aspiring generation, but what he lacked in terms of pure skill and finesse, he more than made up for in determination. By 1973 he

EARLY IN THAT CRUCIAL CANADIAN RACE, JONES'S WILLIAMS FWO7B LEADS DIDIER PIRONI'S LIGIER AND THE BRABHAM-FORD OF HIS CHAMPIONSHIP ARCH-RIVAL NELSON PIQUET.

had put himself in a position to challenge for the prestigious British Formula 3 championship. He lost the title at the final race to fellow rising star Tony Brise, who was to lose his life in the tragic air crash which wiped out Graham Hill's entire F1 team only two years later.

In 1975 he got his F1 chance, driving a privately entered Formula 1 Hesketh. Later that year, he had a few drives in Graham Hill's team – finishing fifth in the German Grand Prix at Nurburgring – but it wasn't until he teamed up with former motorcycle champion John Surtees the following year

that Alan Jones really began to make some serious headway.

He first attracted attention at the wheel of the neat Surtees TS19 when he ran ahead of James Hunt's McLaren to lead the early stages of the Race of Champions at Brands Hatch, eventually finishing second to the man who

would go on to win the World Championship later the same season.

Unfortunately, the relationship between Surtees and Jones was never as easy as both men would have hoped. John himself was a previous World Champion, having taken the seven titles on two wheels before switching to cars and winning the 1964 title for Ferrari. He could be a stern taskmaster and had very fixed ideas about how to operate a Grand Prix team. These did not always sit easily with Jones's outspoken and candid approach, so when Alan ventured any criticism of the TS19 – however mild – it often provoked a frosty reaction from his employer.

At the end of 1976, Jones left Surtees, uncertain what he would do next. A career in the second-division Formula 5000 category, racing in the United States, was one of the possibilities, but a set of tragic circumstances presented him with the chance to continue on the F1 stage. Welsh driver Tom Pryce was killed at the wheel of his Shadow DN8 in the South African Grand Prix at Kyalami and Jones was invited to replace him. Within months, Jones had demonstrated his true potential with a well-judged victory in the rain-soaked Austrian Grand Prix, taking the lead when James Hunt's McLaren rolled to a halt with engine failure.

A DAY TO SAVOUR: JONES FACES THE MICROPHONES AFTER CLINCHING THE 1980 WORLD CHAMPIONSHIP WITH A VICTORY IN THE CANADIAN GP AT MONTREAL.

His success was noted by Frank Williams, then struggling to establish his second F1 team after selling the financially battered remains of his previous organization to Walter Wolf, later entrant for Jody Scheckter in 1977. Williams picked up the threads again with a private March-Ford, but had ambitious plans to build his own car in 1978, which would be designed by former Wolf engineer Patrick Head who had joined his new project from the outset.

Williams Grand Prix Engineering began to establish itself as a serious F1 force in 1978 with Alan Jones driving the team's sole entry in the World Championship. It was a classic case of three talented individuals coming together just at the right moment: Frank was poised to shrug aside his image as something of an F1 muddler, Head had designed a compact, promising chassis and Jones was ready to give it his best shot from behind the wheel.

The combination of Jones and the agile Williams FW06 proved extremely promising. Both car and driver were quick enough to pose a competitive threat, but the team was suffering from a rash of technical failures and general unreliability, which hindered its efforts to establish a solid reputation. But Jones ended the season on a high, finishing second to Carlos Reutemann's Ferrari in the United States Grand Prix. And, Patrick Head was intent on following Lotus chief Colin Chapman's lead by designing a car to exploit ground effect aerodynamics the following year, so Jones and Williams were on their way to the Big Time.

The new Williams FW07 was introduced in time for the 1979 Spanish Grand Prix. It would eventually prove one of the season's front runners and enabled Jones to firmly establish his position in the front rank of Formula 1 competition. This was also the first season in which Williams GPE had run two cars, the second entrusted to veteran Swiss Clay Regazzoni. It was somewhat ironic that it fell to Clay to score the first Williams win in the British Grand Prix at Silverstone, although Jones had been comfortably ahead throughout — until a leaking water pump forced him into retirement.

Jones only had to wait a fortnight before scoring his first win for the team in Germany. Once into his stride, he added the Austrian, Dutch and Canadian races to his victory tally, finishing the year by taking third place in the Drivers' World Championship. Somehow, the Grand Prix community sensed that he was ready to challenge for the title the following year. He was, and he did.

By this time, Williams had been able to secure considerable sponsorship from a variety of Saudi Arabian commercial and business interests, which included Saudia, the Kingdom's national airline, Albilad, the Saudi Royal family's official trading company, and TAG — Techniques d'Avante Garde — a Paris-based international trading company with interests in industries ranging from aerospace to military equipment. TAG had been founded by a wealthy Lebanese businessman, Akram Ojjeh, whose most famous business coup had been brokering the sale of the huge transatlantic liner *France* from the French Line to a Norweigan cruise company.

Ojjeh's eldest son Mansour took a keen interest in TAG's sponsorship of the Williams team and quickly became a close friend of Frank, Patrick and Alan. The team was extremely well financed as a result of this backing, yet one never formed the impression that the key players were living lavishly on the back of their newly found wealth. For the

SOMEHOW, THE GRAND PRIX COMMUNITY SENSED THAT HE WAS READY TO CHALLENGE FOR THE TITLE THE FOLLOWING YEAR

JONES IN THE COCKPIT OF HIS WILLIAMS FW07B: A MAN AS TOUGH AS HIS CAR.

Williams team, this access to ample funding meant that there was more money to invest in high technology, racing engines and any engineering advantage which might sharpen the team's competitive edge. Grand Prix motor racing remained the total priority.

In 1980, Jones scored five Grand Prix victories and snatched the Championship at Montreal in the penultimate race of the season, edging out a challenge from his arch-rival Nelson Piquet. Jones, the tough guy, had little time for Piquet on a personal level and gained enormous satisfaction from this success. In reality, the contrast between the two men was well defined.

On a race just before the Championship decider, one observer remarked that the sight of Jones in his dark green racing overalls was reminiscent of a military helicopter pilot off on a mission in Vietnam. Nelson, on the other hand, looked like a jockey about to be helped onto his horse. This may have been a gross simplification of the relative merits of the two drivers, but Jones certainly looked the more intimidating as he was strapped into the cockpit of his Williams.

Jones ended his title season with earnings comfortably in excess of the $1 million mark – and he would earn more again as reigning Champion the following year. But the influx of more finance into the Williams coffers had obliged the team to run two ace drivers from 1980 onwards, so the easy-going Regazzoni was replaced by Carlos Reutemann.

An introspective Argentinian who had a deeply analytical approach to motor racing, Reutemann was no more Jones's cup of tea than Piquet. Although Alan was no fool, he had a markedly less esoteric approach to driving Grand Prix cars. If they didn't want to be manhandled into submission, then there was obviously a problem and the team could damn well sort it out. Not for AJ the obsessive fiddling with chassis settings, just

a desire to get out onto the circuit as quickly as possible and blitz the opponents into submission.

Jones should have retained his World Championship in 1981, but mechanical problems robbed him of a decisive victory in the German GP and a possible win at Silverstone evaporated in a first lap collision with Villeneuve's spinning Ferrari. He also reasoned he was robbed of victory in Brazil, when Reutemann beat him into second place by steadfastly ignoring pit signals that he should drop back behind the Australian. The general mood in the Williams garage after the event was definitely not improved by this indiscipline and added further to the tensions existing between the two men.

At the end of 1981 Jones decided to retire. He had a romantic notion of returning to his native Australia, to a life of farming, beer and barbecues. But it didn't take long before he was back racing in national sports car championship events with a Porsche turbo and, four years later, he would be back on the F1 scene when the giant US foods and consumer products conglomerate, Beatrice, bankrolled the lavish Lola-Ford team run by Chicago entrepreneur Carl Haas.

Jones reputedly received $6 million for an 18-month commitment. It was an offer that was to good to resist. But there was absolutely no question of re-kindling the past glory of his Williams days. The Lola-Fords proved inconclusively competitive and Jones retired from F1 for good at the end of 1986, financially well qualified for the retired World Champion Millionaire's club.

IN 1980, JONES SCORED FIVE GRANDS PRIX VICTORIES AND SNATCHED THE CHAMPIONSHIP AT MONTREAL IN THE PENULTIMATE RACE OF THE SEASON

DURING HIS ASSAULT ON THE 1980 CHAMPIONSHIP, JONES FAVOURED THESE DARK GREEN OVERALLS. SOMEHOW THEY ADDED TO HIS TOUGH-GUY IMAGE.

Had his father's ambitions won out, Nelson Piquet might well have made his international reputation on the centre court at Wimbledon rather than on the shimmering tarmac at Buenos Aires, Barcelona and Brands Hatch. Born in Rio de Janeiro on 17 August, 1953, he initially followed in his father's footsteps to become an accomplished tennis player. He was even packed off to California by his family for an intensive programme of coaching before his they capitulated and the lure of cars, karts and motorcycles took his complete attention.

Nelson began racing cars seriously in the Brazilian national Super Vee championship, driving basic single-seater machines that were powered by lightly turned Volkswagen engines. In 1977 he set out for Europe to try his hand in the continental F3 championship before coming to Britain to tackle the national series in 1978. He quickly established himself as a dominant force in that category, winning no fewer than 13 races during the course of a hectic year.

Piquet's obvious talent quickly earned him a place on the lower rungs of the F1 ladder. He made his Grand Prix debut for the minor-league Ensign team at Hockenheim and then drove a private McLaren in the Austrian, Dutch and Italian races. After that, he was invited to take the wheel of one of the works Brabham-Alfa Romeos in the Canadian race at Montreal.

Bernie Ecclestone, the shrewd Brabham team chief, signed up Nelson on a three-year contract from the start of 1979. Initially he was set to partner Niki Lauda, but when the Austrian abruptly retired midway through practice in Canada, Nelson found himself thrust into the team leadership role in his first full season of F1. Unquestionably, he was well up to the task. In 1980 he won his first Grand Prix at Long Beach, continuing to score further victories in the Dutch and Italian races, and came within striking distance of beating Alan Jones to the World Championship at the end of the year.

In 1981 he won what would be the first of his three Championship crowns, edging out Carlos Reutemann in the final race of the year at Las Vegas. The following year saw Brabham swap its trusty 3-litre Ford V8 engines for a deal with BMW to use the German company's massively powerful, but initially unreliable, turbocharged four-cylinder units. He managed only a single win that year, but came back to take his second championship in 1983.

By now, Nelson felt very much at home within the Brabham team enclave. He was enormously popular with the mechanics who

regarded him as one of their own. There was nothing pompous about Piquet; he was just crazy about cars and motor racing. One might have been forgiven for concluding that this was his abiding true love had it not been for his increasingly complex off-track personal life, which saw him father several children – all of whom he absolutely and unreservedly adored – by three stunningly attractive lady friends.

After winning his second title, two rather bleak years followed with the Brabham-BMW team, during which Piquet managed to win only three races. The inconsistent performances produced by the team during this period was, in part, due to the fact that Ecclestone had signed a lucrative tyre supply contract with Pirelli at the start of 1984 – and the Italian tyre-maker's products were no match for the Goodyears used by all the other top teams.

Even so, the bond that existed between Piquet, Ecclestone and the Brabham team seemed sufficiently strong that it was hard to imagine him driving for another team. With that in mind, the F1 world was stunned when he decided to leave the team to join Williams in 1986, partly attracted by the prospect of using powerful Honda engines – and partly by the fact that Frank was prepared to pay around $2 million for his services. Reputedly, this was almost twice Bernie's final bid to retain his services.

Williams had been anxious to sign Piquet as Keke Rosberg had indicated he would be switching to the McLaren camp for 1986. At the time, Frank was about midway through his first season with Nigel Mansell as his second driver, but the Englishman had yet to prove conclusively that he was of a calibre which would yield a consistent flow of race wins. Yet by the end of the season, Nigel had come on in leaps and bounds and it was clear that he was aiming to beat Piquet fair and square come the start of 1986.

Nelson could have been forgiven for thinking Mansell would be a push-over when, in the first race at Rio, Nigel was bundled off the circuit in a collision with Ayrton Senna's Lotus-Renault. Piquet thereafter stroked his way easily to a memorable home victory, unaware what surprises lay a little further down the Championship trail.

Put simply, Mansell really got his act together with the Williams-Honda FW1 and began to fly, reeling off victory after victory early on in the summer of 1986. More frustratingly for Nelson, the Williams management didn't seem to be interested in keeping Mansell under control. The Brazilian believed it was a term of his contract as team leader that his colleague would defer to him out on the circuit. Not so, argued Williams. Nelson had priority access to the spare car, but no special deals when it came to the racing.

The seriousness of this situation got badly out of focus in Nelson's mind and no constraints prevented him from discussing the matter with the Williams team. On his way to Nice airport after the final pre-season test at Paul Ricard, Frank Williams was involved in a serious car accident which left him paralysed from the chest down. For much of 1986 he was in hospital, fighting to regain as much mobility as possible. This was not, Nelson rightly reasoned, the best moment to start arguing about his status within the team.

However, the Williams strategy of allowing its drivers to race each other with as much gusto as the opposition had negative results: neither man won the Championship. Put simply, they robbed each other of sufficient points so as to permit Alain Prost to dodge

> **AFTER WINNING HIS SECOND TITLE, TWO RATHER BLEAK YEARS FOLLOWED WITH THE BRABHAM-BMW TEAM, DURING WHICH PIQUET MANAGED TO WIN ONLY THREE RACES**

EXHAUSTED. NEAR TO COLLAPSE AFTER WINNING THE **1981** BRAZILIAN GRAND PRIX AT RIO, PIQUET WAS SUBSEQUENTLY DISQUALIFIED WHEN HIS BRABHAM-FORD WAS DEEMED TO HAVE INFRINGED THE TECHNICAL RULES.

NELSON'S VICTORY IN THE 1987 ITALIAN GRAND PRIX AT MONZA, THE FIRST FOR THE ACTIVE SUSPENSION WILLIAMS-HONDA FW11B, REPRESENTED A CRUCIAL STEP TOWARDS HIS THIRD CHAMPIONSHIP TITLE.

through at the last race to hang on to the championship he had won the previous year. Unfortunately, this debacle was acted out under the critical eye of Honda patriarch Soichiro Honda. To all intents and purposes, it marked the beginning of the end of the Williams-Honda partnership, which was dissolved at the end of 1987 – despite the fact that, contractually, it still had a year to run.

Despite Mansell's sustained competitive

On the opening lap of the 1987 Italian GP he leads Nigel Mansell's Williams-Honda, Gerhard Berger's Ferrari, Ayrton Senna's Lotus-Honda and Alain Prost's McLaren down Monza's long back straight into the tricky Parabolica right-hander.

edge, Piquet came out of 1987 with his third World Championship. This achievement was made all the more remarkable by the fact he had suffered for much of the season with the effects of a huge 190-mph-accident during practice for the San Marino GP at Imola. For some months he confessed he could not sleep properly and felt generally disorientated. Yet, by sticking relentlessly to his philosophy that one must finish as many races as possible in order to have a crack at the championship – a very logical viewpoint he shared with his one-time team-mate Niki Lauda – Nelson came out on top at the end of the year.

He had enjoyed his time with Williams, no question, but now he judged it was time to

move on – to Lotus, where he would continue to enjoy all the benefits of a Honda engine supply contract, number one status and a retainer in the order of $4 million from the team's sponsors, the R. J. Reynolds cigarette conglomerate.

During his time with Williams, Nelson's greatest strength had been his appetite for test and development work. He liked nothing more than developing some new technical accessory away from the spotlight of a Grand Prix weekend – and then going to the start of the next race secure in the knowledge that he had a potential performance advantage under his belt. He was also very assiduous and reasoned in his approach to pre-race testing; he knew that absolute, shattering lap times were not always totally relevant. Instead, he preferred to work on the race set-up of his cars and keep his knowledge to himself, rather like a poker player who knows he has a winning hand.

By the time he left Williams, Nelson Piquet had won no fewer than 23 Grands Prix. But his two-year tenure with Lotus proved bleak and relatively unproductive. From the heights of World Champion in 1987, he slumped to sixth in the final points table the following year, then down to eighth in 1990. And in neither of those seasons was he able to score a single race win.

Yet Piquet remained convinced that he could still deliver competitive results in the right car, even though his perceived status had suffered from his apparent poor-showing with Lotus. He landed a seat with Benetton-Ford in 1990, reputedly for a modest retainer, which would be topped up with a bonus of around $12,000 for every Championship point

> **DESPITE MANSELL'S SUSTAINED COMPETETIVE EDGE, PIQUET CAME OUT OF 1987 WITH HIS THIRD WORLD CHAMPIONSHIP**

scored. If that really was the case, then Nelson would have finished the season with a smile on his bank manager's face. He won the final races of the season, in Japan and Australia, scoring 18 points in a fortnight to boost his income by over $200,000!

Nelson scored his final Grand Prix victory in the 1991 Canadian Grand Prix before being dropped from the Benetton line-up in favour of Michael Schumacher the following year. In 1992, he decided to try his hand at the Indianapolis 500, but crashed heavily in

practice and sustained serious foot injuries which effectively heralded the end of his front line motor racing career.

By that time he was a millionaire several times over, complete with a luxury yacht in the Mediterranean equipped with a helicopter pad for instant commuting.

For many years he had also been involved in wide-ranging charity work in his native Brazil, helping destitute and underprivileged children in a discreet manner which never drew attention to his own celebrity status.

DISTANT AND THOUGHTFUL: NELSON DURING HIS SUCCESSFUL 1987 SEASON, WHICH WAS HIS SECOND AND LAST WITH THE WILLIAMS TEAM.

Keke ROSBERG 1982

RIGHT; ROSBERG ON THE WAY TO HIS FINAL GRAND PRIX VICTORY IN ADELAIDE, 1985, WITH THE WILLIAMS-HONDA FW10.

OUTGOING AND EXTROVERT, ROSBERG WAS A HARD AND UNYIELDING COMPETITOR ON TRACK AND IMMENSELY LOYAL TO THOSE HE ELECTED TO BEFRIEND OFF IT.

He was born Keijo Rosberg in Stockholm, the son of a Finnish veterinary surgeon, but quickly styled himself 'Keke' – reasoning that the European motor racing press would probably make less of a mess when it came to spelling! In many ways, that just summed Rosberg up; he always had an underlying confidence that he would make the Big Time. He was cocky, but attractively so. Much like Jackie Stewart, Rosberg quickly developed a self-deprecating sense of humour. He could laugh at himself,

so those who worked with him were prepared to forgive almost anything.

Rosberg's motor racing career started in the wake of a disappointing stint in higher education. He had originally hoped to get into Helsinki University to study dentistry, but could not get a place and instead began working for an American company as a computer systems analyst in 1969. By then, he had already been karting for four years. He continued until 1972, when he switched to Formula Super Vee, mostly in Europe, before finally making his presence felt on the UK motor racing scene as late as 1975.

A promising test in a British Formula 5000 Lola for the McKechnie team alerted team manager John Thornburn – already a Nigel Mansell devotee – as to Rosberg's latent potential. But the Finn decided instead to try the European F2 scene in 1976, albeit in a pretty uncompetitive car. The turning point in his professional career came when he fell in with American entrepreneur Fred Opert, former driver turned wheeler-dealer who had become one of the most promising team owners in this second division formula.

At the end of 1976 Opert was sufficiently impressed by Keke's promise to offer him a drive in the New Zealand Formula Atlantic championship, where Rosberg won three of the four races. Rosberg drove for Opert through 1977 in a variety of races. He always insisted on receiving a fair wage for the job and recalls that some of his trips – perhaps to a Formula Atlantic race in rural Canada – involved Opert peeling off a wad of airline ticket coupons from the stock he always seemed to keep in his briefcase. The resulting trip involved about three stop-overs and a flight which seemed to last twice as long as necessary. But it all served to keep costs down and contain team expenses!

Keke's big break came at the rain-soaked Silverstone International Trophy meeting, a

non-championship event in the early spring of 1978. Driving the bulky Ford-engined Theodore, owned by racing-mad Hong Kong team owner Teddy Yip, Rosberg kept control on a near-flooded track as High Rollers like Andretti, Lauda and Peterson pirouetted into muddy retirement. Despite race-long pressure from former champion Emerson Fittipaldi's Copersucar, Keke kept his cool to be first past the chequered flag. The success provoked a memorable reaction from Lotus boss Colin Chapman who, on being asked who had won, replied "Ros...Rose...Roseberry?"

In 1980, Rosberg signed to partner Emerson Fittipaldi in the Brazilian's own team, which no longer had the benefit of Copersucar backing. At the end of the season, Emerson retired and Keke started the 1981 season partnering Chico Serra. But by now, the Fittipaldi F8s were uncompetitive and Keke was over-driving himself to distraction

as he sought to keep his reputation intact. Eventually he decided to walk away from the Fittipaldi team, but had done enough to be invited to test for Williams the following winter after Alan Jones retired.

He immediately proved that his instant flair remained intact and was signed to partner Carlos Reutemann at the start of the 1982 season. Having just survived two bruising seasons with Alan Jones, the quiet Argentinian didn't quite know what to make of Rosberg, who had developed something of a 'Flash Harry' image. When asked by Frank Williams what he thought of the new lad, Carlos thought for a moment then replied; "Long blond hair, Gucci briefcase, Rolex, gold identity bracelet....Frank, I think he is very quick!"

The irony would have delighted the extrovert Rosberg, whose chain-smoking habits drove the super-fit Frank Williams

round the bend. Many times you could come across Keke in the paddock, lurking beside the Williams motorhome while he smoked a quick Marlboro, looking as surreptitious and furtive as a 13-year old behind the school bike sheds. "The trouble is that Frank and Patrick have never quite forgiven me for not being Alan Jones", he used to explain.

For all his outward signs of conspicuous consumption, what Keke had in spades was raw, seat-of-the-pants car control. He showed this to great effect in 1982, when he won the World Championship with a succession of consistent performances and a single race win, but more so by far between 1984-86, when armed with the 900 horsepower of the Williams-Hondas. One of his most memorable performances occurred during the 1985 British Grand Prix at Silverstone, when his 160-mph-average qualifying lap had the Williams-Honda FW10 literally clawing the track for grip as he hurled it through the

dauntingly fast corners which abound at the former Second World War fighter base.

His candour was unshakable. In 1985 when Frank Williams indicated that he was going to sign Nigel Mansell as the team's second driver for the following season, Rosberg flatly refused to have anything to do with the idea. He demanded that Frank release him to go to Renault. He had heard from his pal Elio de Angelis, who was Mansell's team-mate for four seasons at Lotus, that the Englishman was nothing but trouble. He also remembered that, after winning the 1984 Dallas Grand Prix in his Williams-Honda, he'd lambasted Mansell's driving tactics in very vocal fashion from his place atop the victory rostrum!

Williams told Rosberg not to be so stupid – and that he wouldn't be released from his contract, under any circumstances. So Keke stayed on, found Mansell really quite a pleasant fellow to deal with – and freely,

KEKE ROSBERG CELEBRATES IN SUITABLE TEXAN HEADGEAR AFTER WINNING THE 1984 DALLAS GRAND PRIX IN HIS WILLIAMS-HONDA. SECOND PLACE WINNER RENÉ ARNOUX (RIGHT) AND ELIO DE ANGELIS SHARE THE CELEBRATIONS WITH ACTRESS LINDA GRAY – SUE-ELLEN EWING FROM THE TELEVISION BLOCKBUSTER DALLAS.

openly admitted that he had been wrong in his premature judgement of his new partner. But by then he was committed to joining McLaren in 1986 for what he flatly stated would be his final season of F1 racing.

Keke signed for McLaren for a fee of around $3 million – big money by the standards of the time. Up to that point in his career, he had won five races and confidently expected to add to that tally with McLaren. He didn't, finding the McLaren chassis difficult to set up to his liking. He was also overwhelmed by Alain Prost, the 'sitting tenant' and established team leader. When he turned his back on Grand Prix racing at the end of that season, he had nothing but admiration for the Frenchman's terrific talent.

By now, Keke, his wife Sina and son Nico, were comfortably ensconced in a luxury flat in a modern tower block overlooking the Mediterranean at the eastern extremity of Monte Carlo. There was money in the bank, a lakeside holiday home in Austria, a private plane and a succession of flashy fast cars.

Yet the lure of motor racing continued to gnaw away at Keke's soul. In 1990 he came back to do a season of World Championship sports car racing with the French Peugeot team. Then he switched to the German Touring Car Championship, driving first for Mercedes-Benz, more recently for Opel. His own team – Rosberg Team Opel – was established for the start of the 1995 season.

His wide-ranging business interests also include driver management for fellow Finns, Mika Hakkinen and J. J. Lehto, both F1 rivals, and several German touring car drivers.

IN 1990 HE RETURNED TO DO A SEASON OF WORLD CHAMPIONSHIP SPORTS CAR RACING WITH THE FRENCH PEUGEOT TEAM

WILLIAMS 1–2. ROSBERG LEADS NIGEL MANSELL IN THE OPENING MOMENTS OF THE 1985 BRAZILIAN GRAND PRIX. SECONDS LATER, THE ENGLISHMAN WOULD BE PITCHED INTO A SPIN AFTER COLLIDING WITH MICHELE ALBORETO'S FERRARI.

Alain PROST
1985 1986 1989 1993

RIGHT; GLORIOUS MOMENT. WINNING THE 1990 FRENCH GRAND PRIX AT PAUL RICARD IN THE FERRARI 641.

THE MOST SUCCESSFUL GRAND PRIX DRIVER OF ALL, ALAIN PROST WON A TOTAL OF 51 GRANDS PRIX DURING HIS ILLUSTRIOUS CAREER.

When Alain Prost finally retired from Grand Prix racing at the end of the 1993 season, the 38-year-old Frenchman could justifiably lay claim to being statistically the single most successful Grand Prix driver of all time. He may have won only four World Championships – one short of the legendary Juan Manuel Fangio – but he had won no fewer than 51 of the 199 Formula 1 races he had contested.

Prost first came to prominence when he won the 1973 Karting World Championship, setting the tone of high achievement from the very start of his motor racing career. After graduating to cars, he won the European Formula Renault series in 1976 and clinched the European Formula 3 championship in 1979, also the season in which he won the prestigious Monaco F3 classic, the number one supporting event on this famous Grand Prix programme.

His achievements in these junior formulae seemed to provide a compelling endorsement of his Formula 1 potential, a fact which quickly drew the attention of McLaren team director Teddy Mayer. McLaren had been going through an uncompetitive patch, but within the first three test laps with Prost in one of their cars, Mayer was ready to get Prost's signature on a contract.

Alain thus became destined to partner British F1 veteran John Watson in the 1980 McLaren squad, starting with the Argentine Grand Prix at Buenos Aires. Alain performed flawlessly to score a Championship point and take sixth place on his debut, following it up a fortnight later with an equally convincing fifth in the Brazilian GP at Interlagos. From then on, things went downhill.

Alain injured his wrist when he crashed after the suspension broke practising for the South African GP, forcing him to miss that race and the following event at Long Beach. Later in the season he crashed very heavily again in practice for the United States GP at Watkins Glen, once more due to car failure. At this point he fell out with the McLaren management, telling them he no longer had any faith in the team's engineering standards. He left the team to join up with Renault – and challenged McLaren to sue him.

After a certain amount of legal wrangling, the unfortunate matter was resolved and Prost left to join France's national racing team, which was an event that aroused a considerable amount of expectancy. Alain won his first F1 victory in the 1981 French GP at Dijon-Prenois, then followed that up

YOUNG LAD: PROST IN 1981 AFTER JOINING THE RENAULT F1 TEAM FOR WHOM HE SCORED HIS FIRST GRAND PRIX VICTORY.

flag. By a peculiar irony, Prost ended up being cast in the role of villain in the public's eye; somehow he was perceived as the man who was complaining, and Arnoux was seen as the hero of the hour.

Alain was reminded of this as he drove home from that meeting. Stopping for gas, the pump attendant confused him with his team-mate. "You did the right thing, Mr. Arnoux", he said. "Prost thinks everything should be handed him on a plate". Alain covered his embarassment and thinly veiled fury by paying in cash rather than a credit card, which would have alerted the attendant to this unfortunate case of mistaken identity.

Despite the realities of the situation, Prost was furious at the favourable publicity Arnoux attracted for what Alain regarded as nothing more than treachery. He toyed with retiring from F1 immediately and would soon move his family from France to exile in Switzerland. By 1984, after he had left Renault and moved to McLaren, the capricious French fans came to regard him as a national hero once more!

Prost was third in the 1982 Championship, but started the following year confident that he was in with a very good chance of winning the title. Sure enough, he took an early season lead in the points table, but BMW stepped up the pace of its engine development programme in the second half of the season and Nelson Piquet really began to fly in the Brabham BT53. Prost warned the Renault engine department that it needed to raise the standard of its game – promptly and decisively. Yet the Renault management believed that he was exaggerating the danger.

As it turned out, Prost held the lead all the way to the final race of the season before being overhauled by Piquet and pipped to the

with wins in Holland and Italy, finishing the season fifth in the World Championship.

Renault had led the F1 field in terms of turbocharged engine technology into the early 1980s, but by 1982, Ferrari and BMW were closing the gap – and Honda's serious commitment to F1 was not far away. Alain started the 1982 season by winning in South Africa, then scoring a lucky success in Brazil, where he inherited the win after Nelson Piquet's Brabham and Keke Rosberg's Williams – both of which crossed the line ahead of him – were disqualified.

But Prost's biggest disappointment came in that year's French Grand Prix at Paul Ricard, where his team-mate René Arnoux, having originally agreed to give Alain the win to help his Championship hopes, reneged on the deal and kept ahead to the chequered

BUT PROST'S BIGGEST DISAPPOINTMENT CAME IN THAT YEAR'S FRENCH GRAND PRIX AT PAUL RICARD...

title. It was a sad end to what Prost regarded as a badly mismanaged season and it was with enormous dismay that he found himself made redundant at the end of the season. Renault's logic in dispensing with Prost's services was incomprehensible. The reasons behind Renault's failure were, in truth, much more complicated and deep-seated than the perceived responsibility of one individual.

He wasn't unemployed for long. The McLaren team, now revived and much more competitive under a new management regime instigated by the ambitious Ron Dennis, wanted him back as partner to Niki Lauda. Prost had no negotiating hand, for there was nowhere else for him to go. Dennis struck a hard bargain, reputedly no more than $500,000 was offered for the Frenchman's 1984 retainer. Alain duly signed. It was the shrewdest move he ever made.

In 1984 McLaren's cars were to be powered by a brand new, state-of-the-art TAG turbo V6 engine manufactured to order by Porsche. It had been raced briefly towards the end of 1983 and all the initial signs were promising. But nobody could know just quite *how* promising.

Any feelings of hostility and belligerence Prost felt towards Renault evaporated when he won in Brazil on his maiden outing with the McLaren-TAG. For the rest of the season he would race his team-mate Lauda for the championship, but there was none of the frenetic, lurid competition which would characterize the future rivalry between Prost and Ayrton Senna.

With six wins to Niki's five, Prost went into the final race in Portugal knowing that if Lauda finished second behind him, he would just fail to win the title by half a point. From the start, Alain stormed ahead into the lead while Niki found himself bogged down amongst the midfield runners. But gradually the Austrian settled into a steady rhythm and picked off those ahead of him who did not

STROLLING INTO THE PITS AFTER A RARE RETIREMENT WITH THE MCLAREN-HONDA.

succumb to mechanical problems. He was unable to catch Alain, but he could finish second. It was just enough to keep Prost's hands off the Championship trophy for another year.

Alain was practically in tears on the rostrum, but Niki was quick with the right words. "Forget it", he said. "Next year, the Championship is yours." It was a sensitive observation, reflecting the fact that Lauda fully appreciated how much luck had worked in his favour during the season in which the two McLarens had won 12 of the 16 races.

Niki was right. In 1985 Prost won another five races to clinch the World Championship

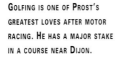

GOLFING IS ONE OF PROST'S GREATEST LOVES AFTER MOTOR RACING. HE HAS A MAJOR STAKE IN A COURSE NEAR DIJON.

title with fourth place in the European GP at Brands Hatch, the occasion of Nigel Mansell's first F1 win. In 1986 Prost continued to keep out of trouble and retained the title – the first man to do so since Jack Brabham in 1960 – after Williams team-mates Mansell and Nelson Piquet spent most of the season taking points off each other.

By 1987 the McLaren-TAG technical partnership was flagging slightly, but Alain still managed to win three more races – taking his career record to 28 wins, thereby beating Jackie Stewart's previous all-time record of 27 which had endured for 14 years. But for 1988, things would change. McLaren forged a deal to use Honda turbo engines – and Brazilian star Ayrton Senna arrived in the team as Prost's partner, determined to assert himself as undisputed number one driver.

What followed was two years of increasingly unpleasant, confrontational rivalry. It started almost before the first race of the 1998 season. It had always been the firmly established tradition that, while McLaren drivers were paid top dollar, they were not permitted to have any personal sponsorship identification on their overalls.

Senna drove a coach and horses through that protocol, appearing from the outset with a huge 'Banco Nacional' patch across his waist, immediately below the team's Honda identification. This left Prost bristling. He'd finally managed to prevail on Ron Dennis to permit him a tiny patch for 'Aeroleasing ' – the Swiss company which operated his personal executive jet – and now Senna had blown a hole through the entire accepted McLaren *modus operandi*.

...AND BRAZILIAN STAR AYRTON SENNA ARRIVED IN THE TEAM AS PROST'S PARTNER, DETERMINED TO ASSERT HIMSELF AS UNDISPUTED NUMBER ONE DRIVER

FERRARI'S MAN. PROST JOINED THE FAMOUS ITALIAN TEAM IN 1990 AFTER FINDING IT IMPOSSIBLE TO STAY WITH MCLAREN AS SENNA'S TEAM-MATE.

Both: A bitter moment. The McLaren-Hondas of Senna (1) and Prost slither to a halt, locked together, after colliding during their battle for the lead of the 1989 Japanese Grand Prix at Suzuka. It was an incident which resolved the 1989 Championship in Prost's favour, and caused a major personal breach between the two men.

Senna pipped Prost to the 1988 World Championship with eight wins to seven – the Brazilian was more forceful and uninhibited when it came to carving a path through traffic, particularly during qualifying. Senna was now letting Prost experience what Lauda must have felt at the hands of the Frenchman in 1984-85. But this was a partnership devoid of any pleasantries. Senna seemed to thrive

on confrontation and Prost felt increasingly uncomfortable in a team environment which he had previously come to regard as his own.

After a disagreement over tactics in the 1989 San Marino Grand Prix – where Prost accused Senna of reneging on a first lap 'no passing' deal – Alain decided to quit the team at the end of the season. His relationship with Ayrton further deteriorated after the two

NEW CHALLENGE. READY TO GO
IN HIS WILLIAMS OVERALLS AT
THE START OF 1993 AFTER
RETURNING TO F1 FOLLOWING
A YEAR'S SABBATICAL.

1993, impressing the Williams team with his gentlemanly professional style, never being over-demanding or unreasonable, but always displaying consummate professionalism, skill and mechanical sensitivity.

Only when he began to appreciate that Williams wanted Ayrton Senna in the team alongside him for 1994 did Prost make the decision to retire for good.

Under no cicumstances did he intend to

McLarens collided during their battle for the lead of the Japanese GP at Suzuka, effectively finishing Senna's chance of winning the title.

Prost left McLaren with his third World Championship, but Ayrton made sure he didn't win a fourth – not yet at least – when they returned to Suzuka 12 months later. Prost, by now driving a Ferrari, was pushed deliberately off the road by Senna's McLaren going into the first corner. Both cars were eliminated from the contest, the title this time going to the Brazilian. But it seemed a primitive method of squaring the account.

Prost spent two years with Ferrari before being dropped one race before the end of the 1991 season. Thereafter, he took a year's sabbatical before being invited back to drive for the Williams-Renault team in the year immediately following Nigel Mansell's temporary defection to the US-based Indycar championship. He won the title again in

experience a re-run of his stormy partnership with the Brazilian on the McLaren team. Although the two would eventually enjoy a personal rapprochement on the weekend of Senna's death, this was probably made easier by the fact that they were no longer rivals out on the circuit.

Prost was genuinely shaken by Senna's death, perhaps reflecting privately 'there but for the Grace of God....'. If there had ever

been any inclination towards reversing his retirement decision at some time in the future, the tragedy of the 1994 San Marino Grand Prix irrevocably wiped any such idea from the Frenchman's mind.

Now it was time to enjoy life with his family, his homes in Switzerland and in Biarritz, and the considerable fortune he had amassed during the course of his professional racing career. For good.

X MARKS THE SPOT. **PROST** FACES A BARRAGE OF MEDIA ATTENTION ON HIS RETURN TO **F1** FOR A FINAL SEASON.

Ayrton SENNA 1988 1990 1991

RIGHT: THE WINNING TOUCH. SENNA IN THE COCKPIT OF HIS MCLAREN-HONDA MP4/4 WITH WHICH HE WON EIGHT OF THE 1988 SEASON'S 16 RACES TO CLINCH HIS FIRST WORLD CHAMPIONSHIP.

A PENSIVE SENNA AT THE START OF THE 1994 SEASON, WHEN HE JOINED WILLIAMS.

When Ayrton Senna suffered fatal injuries after crashing his Williams-Renault whilst leading the 1994 San Marino Grand Prix at Imola, it was rightly characterized by many people in motor racing as not simply the end of an era, but the start of a legend.

No fatal accident in this most hazardous of sports had evinced the same reaction since Jim Clark died at Hockenheim in 1968. But the quiet Scot was killed on a lonely straight through the pine trees at Hockenheim, with only a solitary witness to hand. Senna Met his Maker live on prime-time international television, the 20th century equivalent of the gladiator's thumbs-down in front of the

baying crowd in the Forum. At the moment of his death, he was probably the most famous professional sportsman in the world.

The immediate reaction was a feeling of naked vulnerability amongst his peers. Senna was not only one of the greatest drivers of all time, but also the one who seemed inviolate. Not Ayrton, thought his colleagues. He was the man with the magic fluency of car control, able to ride the outer limit of adhesion, time and time again. The man who could go to the edge, look over and live to fight another day. But no longer.

Objectively, it has to be said that Ayrton Senna da Silva was the most remarkable racing driver of all time. Perhaps he was also the best. Who is to say? Comparing and cross-referencing the strengths and weaknesses of professional sportsmen separated by decades is never an easy task. But what can be said is that few, if any, racing drivers approached their profession with such an overwhelming, messianic commitment as this outwardly reticent Brazilian. And certainly no one has ever combined such skill with a ruthlessly uncompromising appraisal of his own financial value to the teams who chose to employ him.

It is no secret that Grand Prix motor racing is potentially extremely dangerous. But it is not like boxing, for example, in the sense that nobody has ever taken it up as a way of separating themselves from an underprivileged lifestyle, a way out of the ghetto, if you like. Certainly not Ayrton Senna, scion of a wealthy Brazilian family who could well afford to finance their elder son's competitive fancy during his formative years in the sport.

Ayrton's self-belief was so extraordinary that it caught people off balance. After an outstanding kart racing career, he had to have it explained to him that one didn't get paid to race Formula Ford cars. The financial

Marlboro

Shell

SENNA SITS THOUGHTFULLY OUT
ON THE CIRCUIT AT ESTORIL AFTER
HIS LOTUS-RENAULT BROKE DOWN
DURING TESTING AT THE
PORTUGUESE TRACK IN 1985.

transaction ran in the opposite direction. But that harsh commercial reality in no way dimmed his earnest belief that talent should reap its just reward, free of monetary constraints.

After a season in 1981, when he dominated the British Formula Ford scene, Senna found it almost incomprehensible that even more finance was needed to carry his career onto the next level, in this case Formula Ford 2000. He returned home, determined to put motor racing behind him. But the narcotic lure of the sport proved irresistible. He was back in Europe for the 1982 season, taking the FF2000 scene by storm.

It was an experience which taught Senna a shrewd commercial lesson – if you have to

raise your own finance, you should be master of your own destiny. At the end of 1982, McLaren F1 team chief Ron Dennis offered to fund Ayrton's move into the British F3 championship for the following season. In return, McLaren would take a future option on his services. Senna declined. If he won sufficient races, the top F1 teams would not be able to ignore him. That was his reasoning, so he took care of his own finance for the move up into F3, which allowed him to remain a free agent.

Senna captured the 1983 British F3 championship after a season-long battle with Martin Brundle. The following year he graduated to F1 with the Toleman-Hart team. The cars were good, and geting better, but

the team just didn't operate at the sort of technical level that could do justice to a driver of Senna's calibre. He finished second to Prost in the rain-soaked Monaco GP, and third in both Britain and Portugal. But he also got himself suspended from the Italian GP at Monza after negotiating a Lotus contract for the following year without first formally negotiating a release from Toleman.

Lotus gave him the equipment to win his first Grand Prix, in the pouring rain at Estoril. First with Renault power, later with Honda, he would win a total of six races over three years with the famous British team. But Lotus was steadily, imperceptibly, losing its edge. As he had outgrown Toleman, so Ayrton outgrew Lotus. At the end of 1987, he signed a three-year deal with Ron Dennis to drive for the new McLaren-Honda alliance.

During contract negotiations with McLaren, Senna and Dennis found themselves stuck

some distance apart when it came to his annual retainer. Dennis suggested a coin spin to resolve the matter. Ayrton lost and subsequently estimated that the gamble had cost him around $2 million over the course of his three year arrangement.

If nothing else, it taught him never again to be so cavalier about money. After 1990 Senna would not sign anything more than a one-year contract. He paid Dennis back by making him sweat on an annual basis, which enabled Ayrton to set the financial agenda right through to the end of his career with McLaren in 1993. But it was money well spent. Senna won the World Championship at the wheel of a McLaren on three occasions, in 1988, 1990 and 1991. And he never, *ever* gave

LOTUS GAVE HIM THE EQUIPMENT TO WIN HIS FIRST GRAND PRIX, IN THE POURING RAIN AT ESTORIL

RIDING TO WORK. SENNA GETS SOME EXERCISE BICYCLING THROUGH THE STREETS OF MONTE CARLO.

anything less than 100 per cent effort while he was strapped in the cockpit of a Grand Prix car.

Senna's race record with McLaren was absolutely dazzling. All told, he would win 35 Grands Prix and three World Championships driving the red and white cars from Woking. A litany of his individual race wins has no place in this volume. Let it suffice to say that Senna and McLaren-Honda was the car/driver combination to beat from the start of 1988 through to the end of 1991 – four seasons. In 1992 the car was off the pace when it came to competing with Nigel Mansell's all-conquering Williams-Renault FW14. But Ayrton was still a factor, still a race winner.

His relationship with Honda was one of the key factors that contributed to the success of the Japanese engine company's relationship with McLaren. Not only did he take the opportunity to cultivate the senior Honda personnel, but he also went to the trouble of attempting to understand the Japanese social ethos. In Honda's mind, Senna went out of his way to accommodate their wishes. And he had a feel for engines in much the same way as Prost had for chassis.

Ayrton was an instinctive driver. He could feel the car as if it was an extension of his own body. He also had what many people regarded as an uncomfortably intense religious belief, although some people felt his principles had been forged on the 'Pick and Mix' basis, crafting elements from various religious dimensions into a form which would fulfil his own particular needs. Whatever the precise definition of his faith, he certainly did believe that God was riding with him on occasions – or at least watching

SENNA'S MCLAREN-HONDA SPRINTS FOR THE FIRST CORNER OF THE 1990 AUSTRALIAN GRAND PRIX AHEAD OF TEAM-MATE GERHARD BERGER AND THE FERRARI'S OF MANSELL AND PROST.

OVERLEAF: SENNA WITH GERHARD BERGER. THE STRAIGHT-TALKING AUSTRIAN DRIVER BECAME ONE OF AYRTON'S CLOSEST FRIENDS IN MOTOR RACING; HE FELT HE COULD TRUST BERGER ABSOLUTELY.

SENNA'S RACE RECORD WITH MCLAREN WAS ABSOLUTELY DAZZLING. ALL TOLD, HE WOULD WIN 35 GRANDS PRIX AND THREE WORLD CHAMPIONSHIPS...

over him. All of which made him a little bit too much of a zealot for the comfort of many rivals.

For 1993 McLaren lost its supply of works Honda engines when the Japanese company withdrew from F1. Ayrton, furious that his arch-rival Alain Prost had chosen to veto his possible recruitment to the Williams-Renault squad, considered retirement. McLaren did a deal to use Ford Cosworth HB V8 engines and Ayrton began the season driving on a race-to-race basis — at $1 million a weekend. He flat-out refused to compromise on this figure, to the point where McLaren had to pass the hat round to obtain additional financial contributions from its sponsors to secure Ayrton's services for the full 16 races.

For all of his driving talent and shrewd business expertise, Senna could be remarkably incautious. After being excluded from the 1989 Japanese Grand Prix following his controversial collision with McLaren team-

> **AYRTON BEGAN THE SEASON DRIVING ON A RACE-TO-RACE BASIS — AT $1 MILLION A WEEKEND**

mate Alain Prost, Ayrton levelled some critical remarks towards motor racing's governing body, the FIA, and its President Jean-Marie Balestre. He subsequently had to recant before he was issued with the necessary F1 international licence for 1990.

Almost all the race wins that contributed to his three World Championships were achieved from the front, running hard with the intention of destroying the opposition before it could get into its stride. He had a terrible relationship with Alain Prost, but a much better one with the happy-go-lucky Gerhard Berger, who followed the Frenchman as his McLaren partner in 1990. "He told me a lot about racing, I told him how to laugh", was how Berger summed up their relationship some months after Ayrton's death.

By the time of his death, Senna's business empire was as firmly established as it was financially successful. In 1993, the year before his death, he had taken the concession for Audi cars in Brazil. Informed opinion reckoned that the German car maker could sell perhaps 200 units in its first year. Thanks in part to the association with Senna's name, they sold several times that projected figure. His Ford dealership also flourished, as did his property interests and, indeed, his charitable works, most of which were carried out with admirable anonymity.

At the time of his death, Ayrton Senna had been earning around $10 million a year from his motor racing for several seasons – and probably almost the same again from his commercial endorsements and other business activities. He had homes in Brazil, Portugal and Monte Carlo and a British Aerospace 125-800 executive jet to ease the strain of commuting round the world.

CONCENTRATING HARD. AYRTON TRIES THE COCKPIT OF HIS NEW WILLIAMS-RENAULT FOR SIZE AT THE START OF THE TRAGIC 1994 SEASON.

T his was the man who made it to the top against the odds. Nigel Mansell seemed to have more determination than was good for him during his early years in Formula 1, and it wasn't until the 72nd Grand Prix of his career that he managed finally to make it past the chequered flag in first place.

Thereafter, it was as if he had unlocked the door to Aladdin's cave. By the end of 1994 he had competed in no fewer than 185 Grands Prix, winning 31 of them and clinching the World Championship in 1992. History relates that no title holder ever took longer to grasp his crown – in this case, 12 seasons – but

there were few who could argue with the way in which he dominated his most successful year ever.

Mansell served his racing apprenticeship in karting, switching to cars in the mid-1970s to become one of Britain's leading Formula Ford exponents. He flirted with Formula 3, but with little in the way of hard results. Yet his superb car control and total dedication was brought to the attention of Lotus boss Colin Chapman. In 1979 he was invited to have a test drive in an F1 Lotus at the Paul Ricard circuit in southern France.

He impressed Chapman sufficiently to be signed up as Lotus's F1 test and development driver for 1980, getting his Grand Prix break at the wheel of a third car in Austria alongside regular team drivers Mario Andretti and Elio de Angelis. With an absolute refusal to give in, he drove for much of the race in acute pain caused by petrol burns from a leaking fuel cell, stopping only when the engine expired.

In 1981 Mansell was signed for a full season of F1 and produced several promising results, most notably his first rostrum finish by dint of a third in the Belgian Grand Prix at Zolder. Whatever talent Mansell had – and this was a matter of some debate on the part of his critics – it was clearly being masked by indifferent machinery for much of his first two seasons at Lotus. Yet Chapman's confidence in his new protégé never wavered. But when the Lotus founder succumbed to a heart attack in December 1982, Nigel lost a friend and mentor at a crucial moment in his career, perhaps when he most needed support.

He would stay on at Lotus through to the end of the 1984 season, demonstrating speed and flair from time to time but circumstances never allowed him to put the whole race-winning jigsaw together. In 1985 he signed to join the Williams-Honda line-up as team-mate to Keke Rosberg and, just as his critics

were confirming their view that he would never win in Formula 1, Mansell triumphed in the 1985 Grand Prix of Europe at Brands Hatch.

It was just the boost he needed. He immediately continued to win again on his next outing in the South African Grand Prix at Kyalami, which was enough to elevate him to sixth place in the 1985 Drivers' World Championship and signal his potential for the following year.

In 1986 Mansell won five more Grands

Prix, coming to within a few miles of the World Championship when his Williams-Honda suffered a spectacular 200-mph-tyre failure in the Australian Grand Prix, the final race of the season. The title slipped away, as it did for team-mate Nelson Piquet, and it

was Alain Prost who finished the afternoon with the smile of a champion on his face. But that dramatic race through the streets of Adelaide had raised Nigel Mansell to the status of international celebrity.

Back home he was feted as a gallant loser in a manner unique to the British. And while he did not win the Championship, Nigel Mansell was responsible for boosting British public interest in Grand Prix racing in the mid-1980s in much the same way as James Hunt ten years earlier. Yet Mansell still faced a second year cast officially in the role of Nelson Piquet's number two in the Williams-Honda team, and it was not a situation which rested easily on his shoulders.

Although only just approaching millionaire status, Mansell and his family had by this stage been firmly established as tax exiles in the Isle of Man. Not yet one of motor racing's top earners – reputedly

IN 1986 MANSELL WON FIVE MORE GRANDS PRIX, COMING TO WITHIN A FEW MILES OF THE WORLD CHAMPIONSHIP

receiving around $2 million in 1986–87 for his services with Williams – he was gaining a reputation as a clever deal maker and a hard-nosed businessman.

In 1987 he finished runner-up in the World Championship for the second straight year, remaining loyal to Williams into 1988 even though the team lost its Honda engine supply contract. That meant Nigel was left relying on uncompetitive Judd V10 engines in his Williams FW12. He failed to win a race, which left him ninth in the Championship. So he signed a deal worth £2.4 million to join Ferrari at the start of 1989, and raised himself to the position of Italian hero when he won in Brazil on his first outing for the famous Italian team.

Mansell won again in Hungary and finished fourth in the Championship, despite

MANSELL'S WILLIAMS-HONDA SNATCHES THE LEAD OF THE 1987 BRITISH GRAND PRIX FROM ALAIN PROST'S MCLAREN MIDWAY ROUND THE OPENING LAP IN A RACE HE WENT ON TO WIN FROM HIS TEAM-MATE NELSON PIQUET IN SPECTACULAR FASHION .

MANSELL AND PROST AT FERRARI. THE PARTNERSHIP LASTED JUST THE 1990 SEASON BEFORE NIGEL WANTED OUT.

IN 1992, NOW EARNING AROUND £6 MILLION, HE ROCKETED TO AN ALL-TIME RECORD NINE RACE WINS AND CLINCHED THE WORLD CHAMPIONSHIP

a disqualification and one-race suspension for ignoring the black flag at Estoril during the Portuguese GP, a malfeasance which resulted (indirectly) in a spectacular high-speed collision between him and Ayrton Senna's McLaren.

In 1990, by now having built his own clifftop mansion in the Isle of Man, close to Port Erin, he accepted a reputed additional £1 million compensation for relinquishing his number one status in the team so that Alain Prost could be signed up. Mansell started the season with high hopes for a fruitful partnership with the Frenchman, but when Prost began reeling off a sequence of race wins and Nigel remained dogged by mechanical trouble, his mood changed. After retiring from the British GP at

Silverstone with gearbox trouble, he made the vastly premature decision to retire.

Three months later, with Ferrari having organized a replacement for 1991, Mansell reconsidered his decision, changed his mind and accepted a £5 million offer to lead the Williams-Renault team. It was a deal which gave him absolute number one status and the fast-improving Williams FW14 enabled him to win no fewer than five Grands Prix on his way to second place in the championship behind Senna.

In 1992, now earning around £6 million, he rocketed to an all-time record nine race wins and clinched the World Championship. But there was a cloud casting a shadow over Nigel's title glory in the form of Alain Prost, whom Renault wanted in the team with him for 1993.

By all accounts, Nigel now overplayed his hand. He wanted a significant rise and all manner of fringe benefits. Williams was prepared to meet many of his requirements – including another £1 million compensation package for accepting Prost as joint number one for the second time in his career. But the deal fell apart when it came to the fine detail, Williams eventually retreated from his original offer and Mansell, in a fit of pique, announced his retirement from F1. He would eventually sign on with the Newman/Haas Lola-Ford team to contest the 1993 US-based Indycar series, which he won at his first attempt.

Following the death of Ayrton Senna, an approach was quickly made to Mansell behind the scenes to establish whether he might be interested in a return to Formula 1. This came at a time when his second season driving Indycars was hampered by less-than-competitive equipment. Senna's death, which came only months after Prost's retirement, left Formula 1 suffering from a paucity of international stars and Mansell's return was

seen as an effective means of boosting television audience ratings.

Mansell did a good deal, yet again. He asked for – and received – £900,000 per race for four outings; a one-off in the French Grand Prix followed by the last three races of the year after his Indycar season had finished. He also signalled that he wanted to race again in F1 on a full-time basis in 1995, agreeing a provisional deal which would see him paid £7 million if Williams confirmed the contract – and a very cleverly engineered

£2 million compensation clause if, at the end of the day, they didn't want him.

Nigel Mansell rounded off the 1994 season by winning the Australian Grand Prix at the wheel of a Williams-Renault FW16B. But it wasn't enough to persuade the team to keep him for 1995. They had worked with him for too long – from 1985 to 1988, in 1991–92 and again in 1994. And, although the team had nothing but praise for his obliging attitude during those guest outings in 1994, they knew how demanding and uncomfortably

NIGEL'S FERRARI PRESSING ON IN THE LEAD OF THE **1990** BRITISH GRAND PRIX BEFORE GEAR-CHANGE PROBLEMS BITTERLY DASHED HIS HOPES OF ANOTHER HOME WIN AND PROMPTED HIM TO THINK IN TERMS OF RETIREMENT.

After two seasons with
Ferrari, Mansell returned to
Williams at the start of
1991. Here he poses for the
sponsors prior to the first
race of 1992, the season that
saw him capture that long-
awaited World Championship.

FAMILY MAN. MANSELL TAKING IT
EASY WITH HIS WIFE ROSANNE
AND CHILDREN CHLOE, LEO AND
GREG ON A YACHT IN MONACO
HARBOUR.

competitive Nigel could become once he got his feet under the table. They wanted a fresh start, with the 23-year-old David Coulthard partnering championship runner-up Damon Hill. It was difficult to avoid drawing the inevitable conclusion that, coming up to 42, Mansell was perceived by Williams as nearing the end of the competitive road.

Nevertheless, he was still regarded as a sufficiently competitive bet to be signed up by the McLaren-Mercedes team for the 1995

Grand Prix season. By now Nigel and his family had come to the end of a three-year sojourn living in a £3.5 million mansion fronting onto the Gulf of Mexico and returned to rent a home in the Isle of Man while yet another lavish new property was built to their own specification adjoining the Woodbury Park Golf and Country Club, near Exeter.

Mansell had purchased a controlling interest in this golf course towards the end of 1994, but he freely admitted that completion of his new family home was not really a pressing priority. The signs are therefore being interpreted as an indication that the 1992 World Champion, who is estimated to be worth in excess of £40 million, hopes to keep on racing to the end of 1996, at least.

MANSELL AT THE WHEEL OF HIS
NEWMAN/HAAS LOLA-FORD IN
WHICH HE WON THE US INDYCAR
CHAMPIONSHIP IN 1993, DURING
HIS 18-MONTH SABBATICAL FROM
FORMULA 1.

Michael
SCHUMACHER
1994

Michael Schumacher, winner of the World Championship in 1994 at the age of 26, embodies all the perfectionist qualities which make up a contemporary title-winning equation. Aside from his obvious speed and natural skill behind the wheel, he has established demanding new standards of physical fitness, which his rivals must strive to attain, and he also has enough commercial backing to maximize each and every business opportunity which might come his way.

For German fans, Schumacher is their country's first – and long-overdue – World Champion, following along 33 years after the aristocratic Count Wolfgang von Trips was killed at the wheel of his Ferrari in the Italian GP just as he seemed poised to grasp the title crown. Yet Michael's success in the 1994 battle for the title was not easy and straightforward, by any means.

To begin with, he believed that he would not have won the World Championship at all had Ayrton Senna not crashed and suffered fatal injuries in the San Marino GP. He also had two unfortunate skirmishes with authority, which yielded a two-race suspension and two disqualifications.

There were allegations – never proved – that he benefited from illegal electronic control systems fitted to his Benetton-Ford B194. And, finally, there was much controversy following his collision with Damon Hill's Williams-Renault in the Australian GP – an incident which not only eliminated Michael from the race, but also the one man who

might have beaten him to the championship in the final race.

Schumacher also pulled criticism down upon his own head by slating Damon Hill in the run-up to the European Grand Prix at Jerez, the event which marked the German driver's return to the cockpit after the two-race suspension. He may have been badly advised – or it might simply have been a tangible reflection of the huge competitive stress that plagues today's highly professional sportsman – but he subsequently withdrew his remarks and made a very public, and genuine, apology to his rival.

Although Schumacher rated Senna as the most likely candidate for the title of 1994 World Champion, by the same token, it was clear that Michael would pose the biggest threat of all to Senna. Schumacher's great strength is that his fitness beggars belief – his friends joke that when he goes running with his dog, it is the dog that tires first – and his ability to drive every race lap with a ferocious intensity, the likes of which most of his opposition reserve for qualifying.

AND LIKE SENNA, HE HAS AN UNCANNY ABILITY TO CUT A PATH THROUGH HEAVY TRAFFIC...

A key characteristic of every great driver in Grand Prix history is that they have been able to lap at maximum speed from the moment the light turns green at the start of a race. Michael Schumacher has displayed this quality in abundance. And like Senna, he has an uncanny ability to cut a path through heavy traffic, passing slower cars the moment he arrives behind them rather than being held up for a few of corners. This is all absolutely central to the task of laying out the complex tapestry of a winning Grand Prix performance.

Michael Schumacher's father, Rolf, was a builder. Not a rich man. But he helped, supported and encouraged his eldest son to

THINGS DON'T ALWAYS GO RIGHT: LOOKING DEJECTED, 1992.

...OR KEEPING FIT WITH SOME
SERIOUS BICYCLING...

start karting at a track in their home town of Kerpen, near Cologne. Just by coincidence, Germany's first World Champion grew up not far from the family estate where the von Trips family had lived, in a state of well-heeled, if faded, gentility, and the luckless Wolfgang had spent his childhood.

In 1984 Michael Schumacher clinched the German Junior kart championship and retained the title the following year. By 1987 he had won the German Senior title, switched to cars in 1988 and then tackled the highly competitive German F3 championship the following year. He wound up third in the final points table behind Karl Wendlinger and Heinz-Harald Frentzen — and all three of them were recruited by Mercedes-Benz to race in the endurance events which made up the Sports Car World Championship in 1990 and 1991.

The 1990 season also saw Schumacher win the German F3 title, as well as the challenging Macau F3 international, which is run annually through the streets of this

...OR TENNIS.

Portuguese enclave clinging to the Chinese mainland. But it was his speed in the SWC Mercedes-Benz which really began to catch everybody's attention. Sports car racing had not traditionally been a route by which aspiring young hopefuls would chose to lay claim to a future Grand Prix seat. But it served Schumacher extremely well.

Under the tutelage of his team-mate, the veteran German driver Jochen Mass, the bright young star learned all about conserving fuel, preserving tyres and the importance of fitness, diet and stamina, in addition to the most appropriate way to greet and treat sponsors – the people whose companies made his motor racing financially possible in the first place.

IT WAS CLEAR THAT SCHUMACHER WAS A VERY SPECIAL TALENT AND THE BRITISH JORDAN TEAM INVITED HIM TO MAKE HIS F1 DEBUT IN THE 1991 BELGIAN GRAND PRIX...

It was clear that Schumacher was a very special talent and the British Jordan team invited him to make his F1 debut in the 1991 Belgian Grand Prix, standing in for one of their regular drivers, Bertrand Gachot, who was serving a short sentence in a British jail for assault on a London taxi driver.

Schumacher qualified fifth, but retired with clutch failure on the opening lap. Jordan seemed to have hit a seam of gold with the young German, but nothing could have prepared them for the 'dawn raid' mounted by Benetton in the fortnight's break before the Italian Grand Prix.

Tom Walkinshaw, Benetton's Engineering Director, had previously run the Jaguar sports car team and knew all about Schumacher's mesmeric talent in the rival Mercedes. They scrutinized Michael's contract, found that Jordan hadn't managed to pin him down totally – and immediately whisked him away from under their nose. It was an acrimonious moment, but Michael Schumacher has driven for Benetton in F1 ever since.

In 1992 Michael won his first Grand Prix in the rain at Spa on the first anniversary of his F1 debut, eventually finishing third in the championship behind the Williams-mounted duo of Nigel Mansell and Riccardo Patrese. In 1993 he won at Estoril – beating World Champion-elect Alain Prost in a straight fight. He took the season by storm in 1994, armed with the splendid new Ford Zetec-engined Benetton B194.

During the height of the 1994 F1 controversy surrounding the Benetton team, Schumacher showed unwavering loyalty to his employers. There were rumours to the effect that he must have been party to any technical rule infringements – had any such anomalies been proved in relation to such things as anti-wheelspin traction control systems – and there was a great deal of speculation over the speed at which Schumacher's car regularly got away from the starting line.

Michael vigorously denied that he had been party to any wrong-doing. He trusted Benetton implicitly, but did warn that, if allegations against the team proved correct, he might have no alternative but to look for another team.

Even so, he took a perfectly timed opportunity to re-negotiate the terms of his contract through to the end of 1995, a deal which reputedly guaranteed him $12 million for what would turn out to be his first season as reigning World Champion.

The emergence of Michael Schumacher as one of the most successful and outstanding Grand Prix drivers of his era extends the threshold to a generation which will, more likely than not, still be racing at the turn of the century.

NUMBER ONE. SCHUMACHER POSES WITH HIS NEW BENETTON NOSE CONE – SUITABLY IDENTIFIED – PRIOR TO THE START OF THE 1995 SEASON.

GOOD

First published in Great Britain in 1995 by
George Weidenfeld and Nicolson Ltd
The Orion Publishing Group
Orion House
5 Upper St Martin's Lane
London WC2H 9EA

ISBN 297 83528 9

Edited by Laura Washburn
Designed by Bradbury & Williams, London
Litho origination by Pixel Colour Ltd
Printed and bound in Italy

PICTURE CREDITS

Endpapers: Michael Scumacher winning the
1994 French Grand Prix.
Page 1: The French Grand Prix at Clermont-
Ferrand in 1971, which clinched the title for
Jackie Stewart.
Page 4: The start of the 1994 French Grand Prix,
with Nigel Mansell leading Ayrton Senna and
Alain Prost, amongst others.
Page 8–9: Niki Lauda on his way to the title at
the 1984 Portugese Grand Prix in Estoril.

All pictures are © of Steven Tee/LAT
Photographic, with the exception of the
photograph on page 37, © LaudaAir.

ACKNOWLEDGEMENTS

The Publisher would like to thank those
involved in this project, especially the designer
Roy Williams, Steven Tee and Alan Henry, all of
whom worked brilliantly under extreme
deadlines.